Heterogeneous
New & Selected Poems

Anthony
Anaxagorou

OUT
SPOKEN
PRESS

Contents

Foreword

The mystery of life and the complexity of the human condition serve as pabulum for this collection of poetry by Anthony Anaxagorou. *Heterogeneous* is an apt title for this anthology, as the poems contained herein traverse a plethora of fields and ideas, from metaphysics, politics and (pre-colonial) history, to race, femininity and alienation. Although the collection is not explicitly political, the reader can be in no doubt that an ethos of iconoclasm pervades from beginning to end. In the true spirit of dialectics, this collection of poetry establishes itself in opposition to conservatism.

In Heterogeneous, Anthony depicts not only his inner-most feelings and ideas, but also an insatiable curiosity about the wider world. The end result of this synthesis is a narrative which reveals (rather than conceals) universal principles of human nature and subverts (rather than supports) conventional thought. In a world increasingly driven by consumerism, this anthology defiantly rejects the dross. What emerges is a nuanced, though at-times destabilizing, delineation of the flux of life.

Unafraid to grasp the nettle, some of the reoccurring themes in the collection include solitude, marginalisation, imperialism, love, and death. As Anthony will testify, his poetry is not dedicated to the privileged in society, be they political elites or the so-called intelligentsia, but for those who have not been the beneficiaries of societal advantage. Yet this anthology does more than just expose social injustice and inequality. It also brings into sharp focus the splendour of nature and existence.

At this juncture, a preview of the diversity which lies ahead is apposite. In *On Exit*, Anthony chastises the absurdity of materialism: "billboards tell you everything you will never need to know". The spellbinding and timeless joy of true love is addressed in *Not the First*: "Yours is the first body I felt as my own, in your quiet title of simple surrender, feeling today becoming forever, and hours becoming moments". Solitude and soliloquy of the mind are neatly captured in *The Poet*: "Society throws me to the side (I'll make note of that). The people here live fast and hard (I'll make note of that too). I'll make notes about making notes whilst no one notices me making notes...I spend my free time sitting in my shadow just to leave my mind". An attack on the banality of conformity sneaks its way into *This Is Us*: "Money is work-Work is routine-Routine is dullness-Dullness is the majority". And in the rousing *Master's Revenge*, reclaiming lost history is implored: "Don't accept it, renounce it and go back, to before the Chattel, the division and genocide, before the White Jesus...discover the hidden world because history is self serving, self fulfilling".

A sense of wonderment about the material world also permeates throughout: "The majesty of the ocean...an island at ease...lazy olive trees and lost monasteries". A critique of the attempted commercialisation and commodification of love is delightfully depicted in *The Business of Love*: "Of course love is a business...it's stylized, it's airbrushed, it's pushed and pulled, and soldered and burnt...Yet it's even more than that...It's within. It's old and young. Ever-changing. Ever-knowing. It's slap and kick and hold and cheat. It's lust and horrid and animalistic and slowing...So of course love is a business. It's the business of people. Of everyone and everything in a cup. Drinking together. Running lips over the waters of emptiness, in an almighty attempt to assuage the thirst".

Fatherhood and the corresponding entry into life of the newborn are poignantly addressed in *Condition* and *Reflection*. In the former, a lovingly paternal and almost prophetic tone encapsulates the following passage: "You are of no political persuasion. Your agenda is touch... But for now you have done nothing wrong. You live only to breathe, as simple as rain". Eschewing any trite or glib tone, so often associated with the joy of parenthood, *Reflection* delicately unwinds as follows: "Tonight, I imagine each star to be a carrier of wish finding your marble hand. In time you will learn the torrents of your own waters and you will try to unravel the knots of their tightening swells. In time you will learn the nature of the sky too, its infinity and chaos. You must recognise yourself in it and see how you are already a part of its body". Anyone who is even faintly familiar with Eastern philosophy (Taoism in particular) will appreciate the essence of those last lines.

In closing, and on a personal note, I will put to paper that which I have said to Anthony many times, namely that whilst the social scientist decodes the world using pure logic, the poet views the world through a more artistic lens. The poet realises that life is not some sort of problem to be solved or question to be answered. Rather, life is a mystery to be experienced and articulated. Heterogeneous represents Anthony's visceral interpretations of the mystery of life.

Louis Karaolis
Doctor of Philosophy in Law
University of Oxford

For Tabari

New Poems

2014 - 2016

Moon Blood

After much deliberation I decided I would write a poem about heartbreak Stars are We now this comes easy for the neat elegist who scopes out the broken what first don't and slides a portion of himself into the fissure of the fracture gave us the light love from so I did what I do and that is to take my heart and use it to see what our lips an inside to feel out my heart for breakage only this time around looked like shared of us no we there were no irregularities no divisions or stops but now the solid space don't rather only a thing which felt a bit like the moon between them has gone back we put our in if the moon were to be a feeling thing to guard the cycles of the moon side out and smooth and alive with all the light and I'm left living beneath nothing say look my love then I remembered my love thinking of all the light I won't return to this is all I have and how she's restored how singular my lips will forever appear left to give so please each bit of my broken to look I am tired of forever examining whatever you do and with a kiss a touch each crevice of starless street hoping to however you will use me a warm heartbeat rediscover the skins of your silk eyelids the only thing I will ask is to soften the so I went to the furthest point where night that you not be careless with solid space falls into water and I stood with all myself what I've managed to save between asking how many places can the ocean go as I don't have much moon left stars before it too becomes morbidly sick of itself and nights threaten me with dying.

How The Sky Finds Us

I ask

if I could fit my entire past
into your ears

would there be enough space in your blood
to handle what they did to me?

      Is your heart ready now?

Two lovers bounce a kiss
off the space between their lips

      the future is a worn out
      promise

a fatigued pigeon pushes the broken
edge of sky, newspaper-grey
dribbles down another hour

stabbing in fight of lost
ground, hooded youth
worn by locust and wasp

alive to be bullet-shot dead
black gun white fist, silver badge
of fire and force, skin the colour of wrong.

      Graveyards become bedrooms
      where the young
      lay their heads down to dream

in open spirit the prison of earth
melts into stars, the sweet and unloved
hang like lavalieres around the neck
of a tree older than thought

we could list them all like door numbers
we could list them all like genocide
but we won't, instead we will march
them straight into heaven

Trayvon, Eric, John, Michael, Tanisha,
Tamir, Mark, Sandra, Stephen and Smiley.

There is no grave like the ocean

> paper mouths try to close
> off the leak, quick breathe back
> the drowning, pray away
> the flood

pencil boats snap like rage
into shattered fractions,
a thousand lives break from
> within it

lives so giant and small
finding the end of the sea
and the top of a headline
with eyes still fixed on God.

> Council estate manor, drawn to
> rusted meat, licking the fat of teeth,
> lager hands hammer-beaten
> by government cut-throat Tory
> blue razors

tribal hate-march the scum and slag
Union Jacks bursting open the air
like death hounding the royal sails
of weddings and births.

Blame the white collar of canard and fib —
old boy body snatchers remain plenty

Obama death, Cameron death,
Bush death, Blair death

the dying of life and survival of death
sand-graves fresh with innocence,
explosions at the door, in the garden,
by the sink and in the heart:-

home is a body you bury
home is a name you choke on

Arafat, Jamal, Samira, Mohammed,
Mahmoud, Zeinab, Ahmed and Suheir.

They kill all the flowers at once
all that beauty, all that brilliance

all that gone.

Two lovers bounce a kiss
off the space between their lips

the future waits as an unreported oil spill
war perverts the lights

they did it to her on a Sunday in the brightness
of her summer dress, hand to mouth, year to year
only her suicide knew

a boat rocks still against the blue
a flame waves warm under a spoon

there's a solitary eagle
cruising its altitude like a guard

two lovers now contain rain
and the sky stays cluttered with Gods.

Mortal

The dead are made for loving

it's in the grief of their turning,
in the haul of their distance

we live around the only evidence
that one day or night we will add
to the soil

add to the arithmetic of singular chant
and burial,

we who live with the same knowing
as all the dead once did.

The Journey Back Home

I am a locked door,
I am a zip being pulled up on a tent,
I am traces of water being wiped from the mouth,
I am the sound of a headline being typed,
I am the sound of a page being turned.

I am from a time before the birth of God,
3.5 billion years ago when dust found life
and chemicals inhaled each other pompous and brilliant
while sunlight tackled starlight
arriving from some place beyond heaven.
I am the first grace brushing hushed wasteland
and new waters,
I am the first fish feeling the sensation of a wave,
I am the first bird chasing the promise of sky
cutting tracks through the cyclic geography of clouds

I am spreading myself slow like spinal roots
cracking through the body of soil,
I am the first leaf dying,
I am the sorrow rising from behind a sunset.

I am 65 million years old
before borders were nailed into the hands and feet of earth,
I am a dinosaur roaming free the arcadia of time
I am the first constellation being recognised by darkness,
I am the first moon shifting into my corner of night,
I am movement,

I am 14 million years old
I am a season finding the knees of the first primate
which rustled the poised tip of some secret plant,
I am the arm of confident bark,
I am evolution launching itself over all things unnamed,
I am primate DNA charged with the nitrogen of starving stars.

I am prehistory,
I am 5 million years old,
I am a proto-human arriving at the sonorous shores
of existence,
I am Australopithecus settling along East Africa's Omo Valley,
I am the strident rain hounding the delicate calcium of bones,
the prognathous of face,
I am hominoid feet darting to discover safety,
I am the first feeling of phobia but I move through
and so I am the first valiant thing.

I am the moment bones crunch for the first time,
I am the first chimp to wage the first war,
I am the screech to shatter silence,
the first line to be drawn,
I am inside reproduction,

I am intelligence swelling,
I am language in its infancy
and so I am metaphor and hieroglyphs,
I am animism and worship,
I am day and night, I am light and dark,
I am above so I am God I am below so I am Devil,
I am before these things:-

I am Osiris and Ra and Horus and Set.
I am Ma'aht and so
I am Hinduism and Judaism and Christianity and Islam,
I am the same thing,

I am more and I am less, I am the death of light,
I am the explosion of Santorini,
I am a Minoan refugee being captured by a Mycenaean,
I am the birth of Greece, I am a crumb being gathered,
I am the skin Homer wrote the Iliad on,
I am Pythagoras studying at the university of Waset,
I am a black Egyptian teaching Pythagoras,
I belong to everything which came before me

and still

I cut and fight and manipulate and distort
to deny all that I am, all that is me,
because today

I am a skyscraper's window collecting rain,
I am an e-minor cord being strummed in Syria,
I am the tabloid press,
I am the last train home,
I am a west end bar,
I am a broken bell on a night bus,
I am distance searching for home,
I am a cold kerb holding homelessness,
I am a news report burning inside an explosion,
I am the last bit of earth being patted down on a grave,
I am a sticky hand searching for a girl's blouse,
I am the sweat of voyeur,
I am sickness of mind and the terror of spirit,
I am repetition,
I am a frozen auto-cue and I am live,
I am a politician picking dirt from out my little finger,
I am a room where war is signed off
and where water jugs are refilled
and the air-con never stops blowing,

I am a famine in Ireland, I am a famine in Sudan,
I am the opium being pushed onto the Chinese,
I am Tony Blair in 2005, I am Rupert Murdoch now,
I am a prayer in Calais, I am a wave goodbye,
I am a sinking boat,
I am a swollen ocean,
I am a music concert in Paris
and I am gunfire mixed with blood and diesel,
I am a parked car in Lebanon,
I am the number 147 on a Kenyan news report,
I am a tired mind searching for nuance,
I am a wheelbarrow dying of rust,
I am a coffee shop in Highgate and beard oil in Shoreditch,
I am a nod to a waiter,
I am privilege and social media,
I am the French flag flying,
I am genocide and colonialism,
I am selective, I am a protest march,
I am Muslim, I am not radical,
I am not a terrorist, I am peaceful,
I will not apologise for the extremism of others.

I am the KKK holding a flame to a crucifix,
I am a Klan member ironing his white robes,
I am a Nazi solider praying to a dead Jewish prophet,
I am a Palestinian boy tying up his shoelace,
I am a last minute goal, I am the roar of a stadium,
I am the right colour, I am the wrong colour,
I am not white, I am not black,
I am invisible,
I am a genius in Mumbai,
I am a genius in the ghetto,
I am a genius in my mind,
I am a woman playing drums,
I am a woman writing code,
I am a man breaking down,

I am a man breaking up,
I am a solider cursing his grip,
I am a mosquito trying to suck blood from a gun's trigger,
I am eyes looking outwards, I am eyes looking inwards
and I am going to live forever in your mind
and I will govern the banks of your imagination
with the waters of my sewers

and you will shoot me because I am black and unarmed,
and you will wish me dead because I am gay,
and you will punch me because you think I'm weaker,
and you will rape me because you think I'm smaller,
and then you will forget me and look for something else to hate
because you've killed yourself so many times that history
has dedicated an entire epoch to your ghosts

but I will still be here
in you

until the day comes when you remember
that you too were once a baby
who gripped the finger of your mother
and cried when you were left alone

you will remember how your mouth was once toothless
and pure and a heartbeat was the only thing you needed
to make you human

you will think of breast milk and the smell of your mother's skin
and you will see how we share the same eyes
and same nose, the same mouth, the same ears

then you will remain silent
until your hate drowns itself in its own acid rain
and your humanity will breathe in the sunlight
of every summer that's ever happened.

I am a child picking himself up
from off the shore of a Turkish beach,
I am drinking tea with my father,
I'm a Palestinian girl who's no longer just a Palestinian girl,
I am a fishing boat that never needs to leave its harbour,
I am an olive tree that grows,
I am a house that remains,
I am an open window in spring
I am nothing more complex than the bristles of a broom.

I am a door unlocked
and I am falling into a million open arms
while our song can be heard from here
to the beginning of time
we have arrived
and you are by the grace of our heart
home.

Serve And Protect

"Because white men can't police their imagination black men are dying." — Claudia Rankine

If you're selling CDs, we'll shoot you.
If you're eating sweets, we'll shoot you.
If you ask us for assistance, we'll shoot you.
If you're minding your own business, we'll shoot you.
If your tail light is broken, we'll shoot you.
If you do nothing, we'll shoot you.
If you try breathing, we'll choke you.
If you're African American, we'll shoot you
and the world will bury you in hashtags
and Facebook updates and felt-tip placards
whilst we reload

but if you're white, we'll restrain you
if you're white, we'll follow procedure
if you're white and have just murdered
nine praying African Americans
we'll even buy you Burger King.

Doubt

the doubt
the doubt
the creeping doubt
burning everything

Magna Carta

because the land and its sunsets
are not ours to know

because the intricacies of a seed
never belong to the beaten hand

because the perfume of flowers
will only ever be familiar to those few

and because the water
has been torn out.

Stars clank against the steel chest of kings,
the morning frost awakes chained.

The sunlight that polished the hills
stays a hostage to shadows

because barbed-wire fences have been built
to keep those who built them out,

the stone walls were carried and formed
by the broken bodies they work to prevent.

The soil carries within it the exhausted death of labourers,
serfs being tucked down into its melon heart.

Because back then it was written to win
what was lost to the rapacious and hoggish —
to make fair the distribution of life and advantage

yet still the seas could not belong to the oceans they slept in
nor the trees belong to the woods which kept them.

Once there was an intention which perhaps
only served those already named and esteemed

Magna Carta they believed, the Great Charter they harked
into the taut robes of a stale King John;

those noblemen and feudal barons,
their pockets filled with acreage and county

sly as chessmen
stitched their names into entitlement

and so it went, its title and force found the swords
of The Peasant's Revolt and the English Revolution

The Chartists and Trade Unionist and all communities
trying to breathe among the cinders of democracy

because greatness never gets called by its proper name
and everything pledged to paper is forever made to appear

as perfect
as an ancient trick of magic.

The Business
Of Love

Of course love is a business
it's the business of two people or three people
or a family or a community or an entire nation.

It's the business of birds,
of fish, of germs and swans.

It's the love of money, of status,
of food and sleep and beach and wine.

Of declaration and whisper
and promise and gift.

It's capitalism and framed,
it's momentary, it's novelty
and farcical and repeated.

It's stylised.
It's airbrushed.
It's pushed and pulled and soldered and burnt.
Yet it's even more than that —
It's time. It's trust.
It's worth. It's sex.
It's sad. It's peaceful.

      It's lonely.   It's regret.

               It's longing.

It once was, we once were,
it still is, we still are.

It's memory.
It's hands and rings
and vows and confetti.
It's signatures and tradition.
It's dance and song and poetry and breath.

And yes, it's gentle and tender and green and warm,
but it's capricious and insane and solid and cold.

It's dangerous and red and wet and deep.
It's forever and brief.

It's tonight. It was then.
Yesterday. Last year.
Ten years back. Tomorrow.
Maybe.
I hope so.   We all do.

Shit.
          It's without.
          It's within.

It's old and young.
Ever-changing. Ever-knowing.
It's slap and kick and hold and cheat.
It's lust and horrid and animalistic and slowing.

It's shadows and deceit and harm and tears.

It's him. It's her.
It's me. It's you.
It floods and drowns.

It screams and breaks.
It shares and snatches and wants and needs
so of course love is a business

it's the business of people
of everyone and everything in a cup
drinking together
running lips over the waters of emptiness
in an almighty attempt to assuage the thirst.

Old Men From The Wall

A third winter sets on brick walls
chipped with a luck that looks like bone.
I walk a lot these days, noting the old men
who never leave their spot. They huddle
around one another from morning
until the junk grass grows brave enough
to take off its thick white pelt
and the estate can go back
to being an expired advent calendar
the children long ago renounced.

But for the men, where are their wives?
Who waits to hear their stories?
They pack no clues inside the slits of their coats.
Nails stubbed down to the grime, opening cans
with pebble teeth. Blood cuts their faces
like a volley of whispers too loud to lose
again, ammonia leaks from the walls,
from the mouth of the alley where the trees
stream piss, piss leaking from the heavens,
yellow and rancid and holy stinging rain.

Legions of silver breath-cloud crashing chat
of lost bets and fights in their little dark;
there's the swindler Clive who disappeared
last week because he owed money
to some mug from over there or Johnny
who tried dying and seemed to like it.
I want to suggest something but I don't,
relics of the dirty road, nothing Gods
picking splinters from out their hearts
never hurting anyone but themselves.

You

After Charlie Hebdo, Hopkins, Trump and Farage

You're a machine
rummaging the bins for a paper God
searching for yourself in the ripples of sulfuric rivers,
of torn celebrity and vicious blades,
slicing tongues and words slaughtering language and laugh,
shadows eaten by brick and mortar,
wrapping themselves in the hard metal of heated wire
and black bitumen,
the tight fumes of grey industry,
the yellow forest of decay

fuck again
in polished flesh, scented and wet,
lubricated groans spoil the ancient
trajectory of stars,
catch the lacklustre of spirit,
the spilling of mind

You

you're a reckless menace cutting earth,
your pockets can hold only holes,
you bankrupt wings, ruin warmth,
the sclerosis of flight and time,
you unearth heaven,
you point with teeth grinning
at the shape of your dead,
lone coffins sail out towards the end
like pure planets looking for space,
your prisons are not stone and wall
or cage and law,

they are decadence and knuckle
and sorrow and rainbow,
they are atonement and antipathy,
they are you and you are them,
you cut uneven,
your music dead, your stages stark,
your universities windowless,
ill pedagogue, perverse dictums,
yours is a horrible politics
one saddled on exploitation,
           nepotism and decree,
you know nothing of the heart
of the floored and the lonely

your courtrooms are dominated by white wigs,
forged systems of justice and hammer,
the sentence choked in the language of life
           I can't breathe
reach out and touch the eleventh minute for the last time
but it's been the last time forever,
shoot for the police,
for cartoons drawn for profit and blood,
drawn for gun and war,
shoot for freedom of speech
for freedom to pray,
for freedom to walk down the street with sweets
and make it home alive
to grow into the rest of your life,
shoot with poems in the heart,
with fists gripping words like
freedom of speech is not absolute,
because I've seen your people
your hushed and your censored,
your exiled and your vilified

You

where were your cameras and pundits
when we marched for women?
Marched for Iraq?
Before anybody was Charlie
when it was not in our name
for 200 Nigerian girls
for 2000 Nigerian bodies
for Palestine, for Diego Garcia,
for Guantanamo Bay, for the Aboriginal
burning his skin on the last embers
of your acerbic racism
one you've manufactured so well
your finest export

You

will never know what it's like to fly
through the folds of love and compassion,
through the burning vein of another fallen being,
you'll never feel that moment
when your heart for a second beats as something else
you'll never know height,
you spray your sky with pestilence
choke the sun with burly clouds,
your world collapsing under pistons and cogs,
your art is rust, your mainstream polluted,
you live with the lethargy of skeletons
tracing over the faint filaments that flicker and die

you're full of cock and rage
and cunt and spit
drowning alive in whirls of neon,
of electricity you're gone

there's nothing left your children
dream to rob each other of their innocence,
you teach them your greed, your capitalism and your supremacy,
your seeds are bullets precise and intractable,
your muscles are tanks,
your strength is destruction,
your clothes are flags
and your hands
                    are complete chaos.

Yes I know you,
where you come from and where you go,
why you do it and why you did it,
so when my son comes into this world
and asks me on one very ordinary day
"Daddy why?"

I'll bring him in close,
holding his little hand in mine
his chest sill beating and his eyes reflecting the flames
then in that moment I'll confess

because there's still hope,
there's still love
there's still You.

Breathless

She's old, suddenly

her hands shake
her eyes water
her lips disband
her fingers grip
her chest tightens
her throat coils
her head rolls
her mouth opens
her mouth falls

my hands shake
my eyes water
my lips disband
my fingers grip
my chest tightens
my throat coils
my head rolls
my mouth opens
my mouth falls.

The Pathology
Of Like

It was a simple question
he asked to see the picture on your phone
the one you both took the other night
at a friend's birthday
but you declined,
shied away,
said it wasn't a good one,
that you looked too fat and the lighting wasn't right,
placing his arm around you he asked again,
softer this time
until you said "here look at this one, I made it my profile picture
it's already got 63 likes".

Like the time your mother first put red lipstick on your baby face,
crude streams of infant red defacing your stumbling words
like "Mum, how does this come off?"
Like the time you stood in front of a mirror
putting a wrecking ball in your eyes
letting it demolish silently the angularity of your vertical hips,
the burning globes of your breasts,
like you hate this
because your nose is too broad to fit into Sweden
and your hips aren't wide enough to travel south of the Nile,
looking for something to like,
like magazines stacked in your bedroom
higher than celebrity confidence
perfect everyone looks so fucking perfect,
like a sunset happening to the mirrors of a river,
shining bright like a diamond

dream wishing bleaching
scratching skin
because it will never fit into that shade of white,
it will never tan that golden
like mixed-race images
sexualised hair type
subliminal messaging
mind fuck the face
dance
like clothes are made of fire,
naked, look at me
like attention, like validation,
I'm here too
deep, alone, because my body can't do that,
swing sing like that
photographs disliked because maybe I'm
too fat, too thin, too short, too black, too brown, too white
disliked like I can't afford that dress that gets the likes
and the boys saying I like her
click like
like the night you did
and he added you, took you to where the beautiful ones go
to show you their lavish life,
plastic all around
like if the stars get too close to the moon
they might melt
like the moment he kissed you
and you were liked
and it was real and the clothes didn't matter
and your height was perfect for his lips
and your nose could tuck itself into the pillows of his neck
to breathe in his skin
and you said you liked this.

Then one night
he came out the shower and you mentioned the gym
him stopping in the half-light
going over to the mirror to look at himself,
jumping up you put your arms around him but he slid out
like the time his father broke a chair over his back
for slurping soup,
like the time the boys at school
said his teeth looked like desperate council estates
and his armpits were made of immigration
like how could he leave the house with a face like that
smashed by two older kids who wanted the money he didn't have
broken jaw
like when his older brother would watch Rambo and say
"nobody would ever fuck with me if I looked like that"
Bruce Lee posters
stuck over Arsenal players and rock gods,
push-ups in the morning,
sit-ups at night
like the obsession to fight dad comes in drunk
punch
Mum yelling big brother stepping in between
testosterone tormenting veins bulging
like "nobody fucks with me now you drunk tramp"
but violence is for ugly people
and ugly people live alone
like cans of empty cider
like cigarette butts
girls like the bad boys who can make them feel safe like
"nobody can fuck with me now"
but the joke's on him

his life hung in tragedy
like his hair was too blonde to work with that brown
his height couldn't quite touch the tassels of the sun
he would burn too quick

summer stay home
aversion to flesh
tried once to take a topless picture for the likes
but nobody liked
unfriend
weirdo
lonely skunk aroma hold him at night
in white bed sheets he'd keep the window open
to hear the beautiful moan.

Click like,
click add,
friend request accepted
like we're all here living behind makeup and muscles,
the facade of glamour and show,
begging with a damp heart for the validation
of people we will never know.

At a friend's birthday he puts his arm around you
your faces fit the light,
don't smile just look perfect,
add your favourite filter

upload
but we never do that, do we?
Filter out the bullshit
instead we frame everything
that doesn't want us to be who we are
when the flash goes blind

when the curtains close and the show for today is done
when the audience return home to sit miserably
behind the bright box of their silent screens.

Younger Years

I miss the days when I would look up at the sky
and not know how to call it sky

when I imagined it to be a sea dry as tennis balls
that a glide of flying fish had thrown upwards.

The days when I would run around the yard topless
with the figure of a season wearing my skin,

the days when summer could blow through my vest
and time stood as a punctual flower waiting for the sun.

My younger brother and I would imagine
we were both famous footballers

competing against each other
trying our best to score the goals we needed —

in the silence of the yard we celebrated alone
the twilight at last applauding us with rain.

In bed I would tell him how the moon
followed us all around at night

and when he asked me why I would say
because the day had forgotten it

that's why it always seems to loiter above us
as if it were waiting for the moment it could return home

only that day hasn't come and the moon is sad and white
then again he would ask me why

and I would push an inch of sleep into my eyes
taking the universe by the hand to walk it into me —

a universe that could never hurt or leave
or do anyone any wrong.

Trying To Spell Love

There are some things the mouth
finds increasingly difficult to spell

there are battlefields within us
where nothing is able to grow
where our past and its ghosts
search tirelessly for a warm place to die

where the white flags hang over the funeral of God
and our limbs become the mirrored skyscrapers
that attempt to intimidate the sky.

Desperate in our touch reimagining love
through the ephemeral saints of class and gloss
we live away from the centre

stagnant in our wandering
while drowning in the pace of twisted currency
the pace of liquid alcohol hammering our dark veins
driving us further towards the flanks of despair.

Lonely spirit drinks alone
rusted talisman, timid soul
the pictures of the beautiful shared with a styled
loneliness, waiting and wanting for the great ship to return

discovering the beginning through the very fear
that propels the end for love
will only know itself through vulnerability
and needing the body to shake like a collapse
and say hold me here in
the places where it hurts
where they shot me down and left me to die
in the same mudbanks that cull diamonds and forests
listen hard for the ringing of the dead-bells
for the clap of the heart

I'm giving you my wounds because the hospitals are full
and every doctor's hand is a raw coffin
with the insignia on the walls becoming serpentine cracks

so please

bring it here
bring a love without a past or a future
a love with nothing in front and nothing behind
one that's yet to be named as anything that could ever hurt,
one as pure as the dream of an unplanted seed,
as bright as the exact moment a newborn opens eyes
to greet the world from the hot arms of its parents

a love that will walk back through your battlefields
and help bury the bones that protrude from the earth of anguish

that will set sail along your scars
blowing kisses down their crooked river
moving with you
as you learn each other's memories
let hair grow over the parts that pain owns

place each other's breath on the corners that burn
and become the furtive balm
that rescues the deep night from its galloping oblivion

salvage each other
let it all go back into where it's needed

make peace with the waves
and know that the moon tonight
is pregnant with tomorrow's sky.

There are some things the mouth
finds increasingly difficult to spell

perhaps that's it
perhaps that's all anyone is ever doing
trying to spell love with the letters of another's skin.

Somewhere
Inside Solitude

To be quiet and closed
inside solitude

to know its impeccable darkness,
its weighted lung
thrash against the drill
of your poor soul's trouble

> to remain awake only to be mocked
> by the stars sleeping large
> in their bed-sky under the moon's
> historic insomnia

to grip yourself in mid-sleep,
to wake drenched, your nightmare
leaking through, to see the darkness
hacking again.

> Immobile within the brittle walls,
> the grave of all your million voices
> drums in the throat —
> lashes become the eye's spiked cage.

Your hair grows sharp all over.
Your nails dig tunnels.
Your skin's malodorous disaster.

But still you try to give each tear a name,
(knower of all grief)
for this is your belonging
these are your nights

these are your days
spending themselves against such gluttony

collapsing every smile you rightly grew
in such an impossible time

with a dead pig rotting
on the flowers of your heart.

When Grandma Sleeps

The other week we buried her last brother.
She wears black all day long.

I visit once a week now
to find she sleeps more on the sofa.

When I ask her why she says
with eyes on the window
and a hand over her watch

"to be nearer to the ones I've lost —
to reach into a stolen dream
and touch their floating side

to turn them over just to remember
how they once smiled."

When We Are
At Separates

How absent can the blue heart of a moment be

    when your life happens away from mine

    in a place that only cares for the stones in your eyes
    and not those bunched waves I live to drown amongst

that is why my life can only ever half-happen

    when footsteps pronounce themselves in singular time
    and the porcelain wink of a coffee cup rests itself lonely

    when journeys hurry into a mouth with no stomach,
    into the mire of their drag,

    I find myself telling a story that culminates at your lips.

    How absent can the blue heart of a moment be?

That is what I ask when I feel ridiculous
in the non-committal life of my skin.

    There would be more today with you, there would be more
    to watch and press against, and that inactivity of us so sweet

    like fruit, like tea, like steam, like medicine, like warmth
    would teach us the magic of time.

I feel dirty carrying this name
full of untameable woes

into the morning where I'll wake the whole sky
with the only thought I have of you

I shall move past the agony of this blue heart
and speak the sound of your touch into the sun's ear

then in that instant there will be day,
the incandescent bulb bursting over the gloom of the world

and I shall think that today is only today
because you happened.

The Blood

They
slaughter body with bullets,
wound flesh with steel,
dismember limbs with bombs,
break bones with metal,
crush spirit with torture,
cripple hope with fear,
obliterate families with tanks,
deploy troops with flags,
trample life with boots,

they rape villages with screams,
burn graveyards with death,
loot temples with storms,
break history with books,
bury babies with drones,
kill mothers with disease,
kill fathers with smoke,
hang innocence with power,
chain muscles to walls,

but the blood
the blood they cannot get inside,
the blood they spill cannot be killed,
the blood which runs,
the blood which soothes each vein,
blood as silent as blood,
as old as blood, as alive as blood,
the blood knows,
the blood breathes and gives life to blood
the blood crosses an exhausted star to sing

the blood, the blood
will always be made of blood.

An Offering

For Sabrina

Give me your winter,
I have enough ending
to keep whatever that means   warm.

Load me with unfettered soil,
burden me with stone and moss
or chords of frosted glass.

Pour marble-rain into me,
hurt my skin with whatever steals
you from yourself

unplug those heavy dunes
and let the sand drain my blood.

Throw your coldest river at me,
I am drought, capaciously stagnant
dreaming of depth

in the middle of black come dart me
with twitching stars, I'll return you
a whole night aestheticised.

For each fall I shall be there
wanting for you what I've wanted
for myself for so long -

a serving of a good season, a little spell of sun
to taper the shade or in other words
no matter how burdensome the time

the breath of another's
will always remain   warm.

Come to me in your sparkling grace
lay down in this near completed form

heal beside me, become with this becoming
and then lift to fly, my love.

This Is Not A Poem

This is not a poem
and I am not a poet

when I'm unable to find a better way of saying that in 2012
48 people in Great Britain were killed by guns
and 120 women killed by the hands of their beloved partners.

I am not a poet

when I can't find a more beautiful way to say
that no nation in the world imprisons as many members
of its population
as America does

that more Black men in the U.S. are incarcerated today
than what they were during the peak of South Africa's apartheid,
no

I am not a poet

when I can't find clever words to illustrate the fact
that before 2008 Nelson Mandela had been on America's list
of most dangerous terrorists for over 60 years

that Cameron is a liar, that Cameron was a key member
of the Federation of Conservative Students in 89'
that hoped to hang Mandela

forgive me
because today I am not a poet
and this is not a poem

when eloquent words fail me and I can't capture
the struggle of the poor through the metaphysics of language

that by the time Margaret Thatcher left office in 1990
the annual incomes of the richest 0.01% of British society
had climbed to 70 times the national mean

and I don't know how I feel about the fact
that key policy makers and leading civil servants
have never had a job outside of their politics

the same men who set the minimum wage,
with only 4% ever having worked in manual trades,
of which 68% went to private schools

      that is why this is not a poem
      and I am not a poet

because everything I've ever written suffers the weight
of its own futility when another mother comes to a workshop
with a fresh black eye

when there's another empty seat in the place that James
sat in last week and when I ask the group where he is
their young eyes open wet

      as if his coffin
      in that moment
      was being lowered into them

but you see

I can understand all this more when they cut funding to schemes
that are aimed at inspiring people previously inspired by crime
and the insufferable dross of mainstream culture

private prison systems and prisons for profit

when young women are given more options than just
be someone's girl, be someone's mother, be someone's silence,
but you see, I've done it again

I've crossed themes
I've not followed traditional poetic form

    and so I'm a terrible poet

    because how do I speak words in prison
    then tell a young black person
    that they were once kings and queens of lands
    whose names fall dead on their tongue?

    How do I return their history?
    How do I mention The Marriott Excavation?
    Cheikh Anta Diop and the skin-cell sampling
    of three hundred mummies?

How do I show them pictures of skyscrapers
before skyscrapers even existed?
How do I do all this and then have them ask
what part of the world I'm from,
why I don't write poetry about 1974,
EOKA and Kissinger
until I tell them

    that I am not a poet

and nothing I can write will help dismantle this idea of race
that we've become so attached to

nothing I can write will include the importance of mitochondrial DNA
and the 99.99% of us that is identical

that a BNP member most probably has more Asian and Arab in them
than the mosque they conspire to blow up

that immigration isn't a choice,
that people don't come to the UK for great weather,
hospitality and quality of life
how do I explain all this and still retain artistic merit?

I spent days looking for a metaphor to put the Palestinian Nakba in
until I found a home that once stood beautiful and prim
then I opened the door
and saw its contents ransacked
its family massacred and its garden on fire

from that day I abandoned any hope of metaphor
and accepted that I could not write poetry about this
that everything I tried to imagine had already slit its own stomach

like the afternoon I spent with a woman who had been raped
and I asked her to capture it in verse,
I asked her to use simile and alliteration,
until she looked at me and said
"I don't know what those things mean
but I can tell you in a few simple words
what it feels like to live with the Satan of your own heart"

poetry isn't for me

it's for people who can use words like odoriferous
while putting red wine to the lips of their white skin
and applaud the technical endeavour of a poem,
its wit, its ingenuity, its meter and form

not its helping, not the ambulance siren
that screeches from the height of its title,
that is why

       this is not a poem
       and I am not a poet

because I cried reading Douglas Dunn,
Arun Kolatkar, Borges and Neruda.

I cried when I went looking for female poets and found few.
I cried when I asked how many black poets Penguin had ever published
and was told two

when my English teacher told me that language wasn't my strength
that my anger crushed my intelligence,
that I should think about going and learning a trade

and I cried then too

when I spoke to a group of young men about what it was to be a man,
how we inherit this cancerous culture, how we inherit misogyny,
objectification and the glory of violence
while silently suppressing the sensual,

these were all the hardest things to write about,
to talk about and to live with
that is why I keep saying

> that this is not a poem
> and I am not a poet

because all of the above digress and ignore the rules
set by the establishment,

but all that doesn't matter
because it's done now,
you've come this far in listening
endings are always the hardest things to write
because the author knows that's the last impression
the reader will be left with

so I chose the following wisely —

we are made up of all the things that broke us
just to keep us alive

maybe I could have said just that
but I didn't because like I said

> this is not a poem
> and I am not a poet.

Some Place Else

Dad's still sat in his living room chair
banging his head against the block of darkness
he made for himself.

Brother's still planted in front of a screen
trying to win at a game
which needs him to kill everything he sees.

Sister's still planted in front of a mirror
trying to win at a game
which needs her to kill everything she sees

and mum still stares out into the yard
burning her small eyes on a world moving
gone to say goodbye

but the little clock on our kitchen wall is happy

because time is the only thing
which prepares to leave
at the exact second it arrives.

Crimes Of The Land

For Aylan Kurdi

It is impossible for a wave to catch fire
and burn.

There are no mines hidden in ebbing tides.
There are no soldiers crouched in the surf.

The sea does not invade living room space,
it does not erase cultures,
rip out phone-lines or massacre families.

The sea wants healing.
The sea gives salt.

Sharks know nothing of guns or drones,
whales have never imprisoned or tortured,
fish will not violate women
and coral will never call you what you are not.

The sea preserves with its depth and laments,
its single eye a face of ancient tears.

It offers its mass to those fleeing,
those running from what it has never been.

It lives muted as a stretch of life
of future and escape.
Its politics stay transparent, its storms fluid.

With its current it knows why hands tremble.

Fear is loaded and crammed onto its leather back.
People are huddled inside the shelter of prayer.

On slabs of loose floats
it carries those flaring hearts
to lands where the sound of nervous blood
is shunned,

where life is met with tabloid disdain
and no entry and wait

while on the shore fall those the land betrayed,
and like a series of lips the sea's somber crests
swell up to kiss the final mouth of a child
who lays dreamless and unturned in the sand.

From
Jumping Off Feathers

2016

Still Kicking

Her belly high.

      Not long to go.

At night she takes my hand
and lays it over the panoptic sky of his globe.

      I'm all teeth and lips at the feeling
      drifting the heat of oiled skin.

We wish on him through the backs of our eyes,
our worried touch wanting to smooth out his unborn.

What are we still trying to feel for?

A push   A kick   A light

until the ancient muscle of some unannounced miracle
moves like the gymnastics of the primordial and blind

in a dangerous blaze he strikes skywards rattling ribs
she grimaces, grips her flank to howl

steady as medicine
she breathes him out slow.

A softness sets around the pillows of her eyes
and her wire-mouth relaxes

she asks if I'm afraid
      I pull her gently towards me
      dropping the heaviness off
      somewhere close and shaking.

Condition

You have done nothing wrong.

You have not lied or cheated
or robbed another of life.

You have not sworn or fought
or manipulated to gain.

You are of no political persuasion.
Your agenda is touch.

You know nothing of race and class
or sex and faith.

You are yet to learn what a fist feels like
when it grips a loose anger.

Your hands cannot be called hands
they are still two strange motoric devices

equipped with ten flexing extensions
used to pull and hold and stay.

Your legs are not legs. There is no language
you can attribute to their ancient utility,

there is only one block of body which you
will in time come to advantage

along with a pulsing mind which will receive
the vicissitudinous ways of the people living here.

And for now you have done nothing wrong.
You live only to breathe, as simple as rain

and the space within the number zero, but all
is change and I will challenge the forces which advance

to condition you with the tragic malady of human.
But I will do it differently. I won't do it like him,

I won't close. I'll spell it all out.
Hands. Legs. Good. Bad. Black. White. Rich. Poor.

Once, I was like you. I had done nothing wrong
and once he was too

but that was then, before they taught him
how to leave his son standing in a frame of his own silence

surrounded by a breaking world of things
which refused to say his name.

Skin

This skin
survived ancient light and rains,
cuts and skims of backwood thistles,
brambles, foliage and frost
the cold loss of moon,
conflict skirmished on spear and sword
bullet and batched germ,
repeating anathema,
the chaos of seasons
trapped in a sharp tempest.

This skin
once made new
drenched in fluids of the beginning,
unsighted colours of all inside, supported
by delicate hands, mother-wrapped and soothed
in considered balms, tucked in blankets
feathered in affection, the sun for the first time
trying its lips on unscathed contours, baby
squeezing its eyes in the light like a smile,
skin to be cherished and celebrated long

and this skin
has had to survive the burning strikes of whips
and discrimination, of lash and bomb and spell,
the dearth of equality and justice;
felt fire upon its waters, repelled
the ignorance of fools bound to untruths,
handled the darkness with kindling,
marked its floors with needle-art,
the properties of permanence,
resistance and declaration

and this skin
has had to come home to weight
to weep into the unbarred pours of solitude,
it has lost that which kept it warm,
that which knew its scent and trend,
it has boiled in rage, dripped in exhaustion,
sat by the cool depth of a view
until a chill sinks its bones
and time arrives to chisel its initials
into each bruised wrinkle

but this skin also once loved,
unforgettable moments dancing on the castles of fingernails,
around the giant bloom of lips - for lips too are skin
which contain the enamored tongue of two people
trying to forget themselves so as to make room
for one another

until frail hands arrive to bury the skin of those we loved,
the skin of every body born
returning its nothingness to a greater nothingness
and as they depart so too does every shadow their body cast,
every dream their heart spun as those who remain behind
those still breathing through the skin of life
stand to sing one more time for the sailing who are now
all tree and moon and rock and sea and wave and flame and cloud,
and stone and sand and seed and rain and water and sky,
and star and storm and wind and snow,
and glacier and comet and galaxy and drip.

Tissue

The other night I asked your mother
how much she had buried
in the black earth of her reserve

I wasn't expecting an answer, I've learnt
to feel my own way across the citric cuts of silence,
to understand its drawn out grief and paralysis.

She walked slowly over to the bathroom
as I lay in bed looking out the window,
the city muted by the thick skin of council glass.

I envisioned you out there in years unborn,
dressed in the fashions of the season, your mouth
ripe with its colloquialisms and pep.

I tried to picture your home, your friends who too
are perhaps at this moment floating companionless
in the tepid waters of that first great sea.

I tried to hear your voice and imagine your dreams
but I couldn't. Instead I was reduced again to a septic wound
being nursed by the bandage of my hurting self.

Your mother returned from the bathroom,
there was no flush, the tap didn't run,
a crumpled tissue trapped suffocating inside her fist.

In an hour she will be asleep beside me
and the tissue will fall softly to the floor
where in the morning I shall pick it up and throw it away

and I will feel how heavy it will still be,
drowing in the saddest of water,

and I will feel the silent procession edging along
the heavy roads of each crease she mangled into its fragility.

Reflection

I lay a formula of sky in your hand
inwrought with every salutation ever uttered,
every pondering, every clipped tear
contained there in its blue arithmetic.

> The sky is a heavy thing
> filled with the everything and nothing
> that keeps us all here.

Tonight, I imagine each star to be a carrier of wish
finding your marble hand. In time
you will learn the torrents of your own waters
and you will try to unravel the knots of their tightening swells.

In time you will learn the nature of the sky too,
its infinity and chaos. You must
recognise yourself in it and see
how you are already part of its body —

> how you were born of rain and snow
> and sun and wind, of blue and grey
> and all that rages in between.

Open your hand and carefully
with strength bring the sky in to you
and like the rest you will step into life
amidst the sirens of the city's rain

then in years to come
you will feel the leap and atmospherics
of your childhood sun turn away, and the trees
will appear bare, and your walk will slow to a bed's speed

that is when you must remember to move with all your might
and grow to leave your footprints in the last snow
so as when the great sky reaches in to lift you back
you can go brilliantly with all your name.

The Birth

Breathing on flattened palms
long restless meters scuttling down the oversize of her top.

Her hair pulled back tight. Combative. The climbing hour
decorating the mild light of the afternoon's sky.

The room's clean in its neat surround —
a bed, a machine, a midwife and me.

Her arms extended, stubborn and muscular. Her chin dipped
inwards, her eyes biting to recoil against each hot wave,
                each solid sting.

I tried to offer support
the way the books suggested
but my mouth was a bombed brick.

After each splitting surge she would call for my hand
and I would give her a feeble basket of fingers
because she needed to know the ground was still somewhere there.

It continued that way, over the night's imbalance of stars,
the pain real and relentless as if the blind
were hammering a continent on each organ her body owned.

I cooled her down with damp paper towels
lifting away strands of matted hair from her face.
Agony assessing itself on each thread of falling saliva

but there were never any invectives. Nothing foul.
My mother prepped me for the worst but the worst never came
only a low personal hum

like a bee being blown by spring

until the moment when her body released his life
and my legs became two pathetic pins and my eyes
did what they'd been needing to do for years.

The midwife lifted him out baptised in human waters
she lay him across my chest, his eyes open and ready,

both of us staring into each other's need.

He smelt of the colour red. He sounded like a circle.
I put a kiss on his forehead where his skin felt most like lips

then right there
beneath the dizzying spin of doctors, lights, heat and blood
I held the start of everything

smaller than a fingernail
larger than happiness.

From
It Will Come
To You

2013

For The Girl Who Asked What I Was Thinking

I'm still unable to make sense of your small hands
how such light petals can carry so much dead water
there in the lace of their palm's white grooves
maybe that's why you never let me see you
promise anything.

I've often wondered where your eyes go
when they disappear, to that place that brings you closer into me,
your exhausted head sinking on my skin,
touching my mouth with its wet silence
maybe that's why you never let me see your face with tears.

Torn rainbow you are
swimming breeze with broken legs
searching for that last repose, the one found
in indefatigable dreams when dreaming
stopped hurting.

Your way pounds fragility
like an eyelash being devoured by acid
or gorged by the teeth of mad lava
I see you living, feeling, as some unedited script,
one encrusted in the dried blood
of all your unspoken yesterdays

beating raconteur, elephantine imagination,
flinging magnets at the metal of your past,

pulling, pulling,
weaving it splendid into those stories
that are kept in all hearts
            broken.

Here, with me, in mine,
your words rest unwritten
like a blank page living inside a stuck poet's
parched bones,
yes

I believe the future will forever know you
long after even you have forgotten it,
long after even you have forgotten how to read
the hard book of winter
moving far from that swollen fire you call home.

But until then
this is where your face works my beauty
in the high greens and low blues
because the only thing that makes sense
is a love that will never come to make sense
            you taught me that.

So now you see
that's all I was ever thinking
and maybe
            more privately
I really do wish I could lift you away
from the nails of the rain
but I myself
am still filled with so much storm.

Give Hope

Whatever you were doing,
whatever worries were filling your heart with sand
take a moment
        and try to give hope
to the 8 year old girl who's only ever seen
by the broken mirror in her bedroom
and the star-gazed look of an MTV video
that's more obsessed with itself
than the art it's supposed to be representing.

Give hope to the 15-year-old boy
writing his bars on the bus home
until he spits them quietly under his breath
like every punch-line only serves to render
the wide gap in his past
where his father should have been there to say
"son, you're an incredible poet."

Give hope to the guy sitting on the park bench
reeling his eyes over the last text
his only love sent a month ago
like he's double checking the numbers
to some winning lottery ticket,
like he can match all five but he's just missing
the bonus ball.

Give hope to the person who's missed the train
to that job interview that would mean
no more getting up at 5am,
that would mean he could take her
to all those long beaches
they flicked over with a silent lament in holiday brochures.

Give hope to the daughter who's just
left her wet lips on the forehead of her dying father
as his emancipated body plucks those last prayers
from the pale ceiling of a hospital ward.

Give hope the person who's been cheated on again.
Who's been lied to again.

To the person trying to protect the last remnants of their only heart,
who once thought of love as the highest religion
but now sees the word atheist tattooed
on the wings of every angel that only loved to cause them pain.

Give hope to the marathon runner
whose legs shake like the body of his mother's
during those last few hours of her life
whose lungs hurt like the moment they said
there's nothing more they can do for her
so this is the only thing left to do

give hope to the fifteen hour old black and brown babies
born into a system that already deems them wrong.

Give hope to the famine stricken
who crave a full plate of food
while across the pond they fill their bins
with other people's dreams.

Give hope to the ones holding the word of God
in one hand while the media finds a million
ways of saying self-defence is terrorism.

Give hope to those who say
they don't get involved in politics
but who fail to see that they are the most involved.

Give hope to the coltan miners,
to the sweatshop workers and all the invisible.

Hope to the shepherds who dream with their sheep
of brighter pastures.
Hope to the soldiers who keep saying they're just fighting
for the guy next to them but who return back home
            to forever live away.

Give hope to those who have no idea why they're here
other than to supposedly reproduce.

Give hope to the single mothers who become the magnificent face
of everyone who ever failed them.

Give hope to the dreamers,
hope to the risk takers, the eccentrics,
the impassioned and the scared.

Give hope to the person who will go home tonight
with no easy way to say this
            but Mum I'm gay.

To the bullied child whose best friends
becomes the cold shadows that keep them safe.

Give hope to the women
who continue to go home to their lover's rock fist.
Give hope to the men
who continue to go home to their lover's rock fist.

Give hope to the gym addicts whose insecurities
weigh more than any weight they could ever lift.

Give hope to the strong
to those who shout in full voice
not everyone who is quiet is depressed
not everyone with a qualification is intelligent
and not everyone without a lover is lonely.

Give hope to the strippers who've been told
that specific body parts will make them rich.

To the prostitutes who have no choice
but to be exploited by the perverse nature of men.

Give hope to the great sisters who read,
whose minds function as lecture theatres
but with a patriarchy who refuse to turn their microphones up.

To the great sisters who don't need a man to feel like a woman
who don't need make up, eye colour or hair type
to feel like a woman.

Give hope to the dying
to the struggling, to the addicted and the alone.

Give hope to the hopeless,
to the people who you may never know.

Give hope to the poets who throw away more than what they share.
To the musicians whose songs are lost to the thunder of self-doubt.

To the millions suffering with mental health
who live off medication that leaves them staring
into the inside of their own palm
as if it were a framed picture of an award ceremony
that's started to fade.

Give hope to those at the bottom
to those at the end.

Hold out your hand,
let another's fingers fill yours
and take it all in

            then just be here

now.

For All You've Endured

it will make you mad
to the point you find yourself biting down
on your own blood

it will let you down
lowering you into its nettled bitterness
and you'll find yourself bloated with worry (sleepless)

skin littered with the graffiti of your marking past
which you will come to call life
and you will come to call hard

up until the moment it eases
like the hearing of good news
and says for all your troubles

for all you've endured
I will give you to keep
what you will come to call love

There I Was

I walk past it all,
past the simple house I first lived in
where my father's tantrums
raised my mother's poor reticence.

Where his temper quickly raised
two boys with raised fists
who later understood what it meant
when someone bigger raised their fists to them

at school
in the playground
a nose would break

the crowd cheering because the softer boy
with battered dreams under his eyes would yell
as the repeating fists of the other boy
would land with all the weight of his stony upbringing.

I stood wretched
with each break of bone
each drumming stomp

knowing that he and I were secretly related by this violence,
by the paternal fist that taught us both to touch
because on the day he put my surname into his mouth
he smirked,

pimping the vowels and raping the consonants
until I summoned my father's fist,
closed my eyes
begging my courage to stay with me

as if it were the last friend who would decide
not to run years later
when a group of racists would chase us
into the gut of our own fear,

letting myself fall back in love
with the family that had raised us both
I gave him my finest lesson,
rolling on that hard ground,
our shirts ripping, a uniform of blood
schooling us in the same classroom of brutality,

skin on skin
my warm olive against his cold white,
the dying history of my split name
up against the imperial stampede of his
so there we were

fighting back, against the same men
who were bigger than us in size
but smaller than us in heart,

men, who we wanted so much to be like
but who left us with nothing
but the drilling impression of fists

to grow into
        to grow into

intrepid teenagers with clothes too big
and skin too brown
a group of boys moving towards us,
older, stronger, their heads shaved cleaner,
their eyes having stolen to hold prisoner
all the blue from the summer sky

they approached with old fists
with a pace ignited by adrenaline
and a hate they wouldn't live long enough to understand,

my friends running
scattering like fragments of a wish
that get stuffed down the barrel of a gun
then exploded into a dead heart
everyone running

like horses that nobody will ever bet on
all except my one friend,
the one who knew what a closed fist felt like
when it fell like a corrupt hammer of judgment
on a little boy's chest

we both stayed to feel our fathers again,
but with all our crumbling bravery
those boys beat us black and made us the blue in their eyes,
the same blue that could sink waves and drown sharks
only by now

everything had stopped hurting
even when we begged them to stop
because all we really wanted to do was to scream out and say
can't you see we're all fucking the same shit!

Made from the same miserable stock
this is our language, this is our life,
our fathers' knew each other
our fathers' were each other.

So there I was
in a hospital ward being put back together
when my girlfriend came in to sit beside me
staring into my face just so I could try and count the stitches

in those wet diamonds that made value of her eyes.

My friend was OK,
his father was coming to visit
I nodded my head
everything had survived to die again.

The following day
a nurse came in talking about racial assault
she was Nigerian and in the context of everything
that had just happened
                    so was I.

"Racism" I said "is taught to us
because the only colours children ever hate
are greens."

We both laughed
but despite my broken bones and fractured face
I sill thought her smile hurt more than mine.

"Everyone will be black for one moment in their life" she said
"just be thankful it's only for a moment."

Walking out the ward on she went
heading to mend a million more lives
that will never be her own.

So there I was
years later in a school teaching poetry
the class packing up their work
with one boy staying behind,
the same boy who throughout the term
hadn't said a single word
because his accent was too fresh,

things didn't sound right when he said them,
all the words he had ever learnt
had only come to let him down.

He approached my desk with a plain sheet of paper
catching sight of his hands I saw his knuckles were split
bulging with a raw purple
like the fruit that grows from the soil of a graveyard
or a war zone.

I remarked that the page was blank
he nodded saying
"I know sir, but so are the best metaphors
and that special poetry that only fists can heal."

It Will Come To You

Love will come to you
I'm sure of that.

It will come to you
as you are counting the last few breaths
of your life's hope,
as the final feeling in your body
rolls itself into a long purple numbness,
as the alcohol becomes honey
and your only song sinks into stone.

It will come to you
as you sit exhausted on the lips of water
waiting to be kissed by its gorgeous suicide,
when each night feels like a war
reinventing itself in your bones
and every bit of sad news
was written by your hand.

It will come to you
just before you leave, just before you pack
your past away and leave the future
to those whose eyes own it,
when there is nothing left but damp space
nothing left but limp memories to live amongst
as the great earth stretches itself out before you
inviting you with end to die in its stillness.

It will come to you
I'm sure of that, and fly a kite on your wounds
to which you will curl the final tear
around your finger, open your arms
and hold your love, as if it were the last branch
reaching out from the side of a giant mountain
and you've been falling your whole life.

It will come to you
in the same way it left you
(unexpected)
with your shivering heart throwing itself
to the lightning

blind
        thunderous
              and mad.

Hurt People

She thought you would be different,
she hoped that you would never do
what he did to her
and you never thought you could do
what she did to you back to her

especially because the first few months were unbelievable
you would see her and she would hold you
without arms or words or contact
she would just hold you
and you couldn't understand why

when you went to sleep each night
her name stretched itself across the mirrors of your dreams
and you would wake up to see her breathing
like a gentle cloud beside you
regardless of the fact
that she wasn't.

You could feel it growing into something serious
something different
especially when every other woman you looked at
seemed to not matter
seemed to be just another person walking by
not a goal or an object or an icon of desire
but just another person walking with the minutes of their life.

You'd never held a woman's hands for as long as you did hers,
you'd never paid so much attention
to the way her curves would dominate a dress

you would think of precipitous mountains
dressed in nature's green,
you would think of everything with a bend
roads, oceans and shapes that you could touch
over and over again.

You knew what a woman's eyes looked like
when she said I'm falling in love with you
but you'd never felt the sting in your own
when you said it back.

You'd never thought your voice could work so softly,
you'd never taken a second to see what your naked chest
looked like through the moon's magic, her hair blanketing you,
her skin lending you its truth
one that felt like peace as you remember thinking to yourself
that this must be what God's garden must breathe like

but you were a long way from the right side of heaven
and you knew it
because you couldn't leave what she did to you
before you met her, years before,
when you were still soft and love was supposed to be forever
and promises really were supposed to work

before you read that message that was so foul
that you vomited on your new shirt
before she broke you and ran away
with the half that could have been saved
before she stole the boy
and left the man to get old.

You knew all this
because on the evening she spoke
about all the dishonest things he did to her

how he held her in his arms after coming in from her house
how he had kissed her on the forehead with sore lips
glossy and perfumed
how they had taken pictures together
that she would frame over the bed
just so he could bring her back and fuck her beneath them
while the happiness in her eyes was forced to watch on
frozen

she told you all this and you listened and nodded
in the same way he did when she told him
about the man who last lost her
saying men
are masters at hurting us differently in the same place
you didn't know where to put your eyes
you could feel the sweat march across your cool
like an army of invaders
and you knew she had been here so many times before
that she could read your look
like the sky can read an imminent thunderstorm
she let go of your hand
to put hers over her mouth
and she sobbed and sobbed and sobbed
like she did with him and him and him
until finally she left the room
leaving you to sit and think
about her and her and her.

She's moved away now
you heard from the others that it all got too much
she just couldn't be around your type any longer.

The friend who introduced you both
said that in her photographs she smiles a lot more now,
she has albums of all her new memories
bright and filled with permanent sunshine

in beautiful places where people hold hands
to eat ice-cream in the sun.

You nod your head
in the way you did the night she left you

you go back to your flat to look for a camera,
a good camera, because the one on your phone
hurts too much

after an hour of searching
you find one sitting with dust
in some old box without a label

       broken
       and empty.

From
A Difficult
Place To
Be Human

2013

Football Results

As a boy my father took silence over talk,
he would sit deep inside his glasses
as if admiring their stillness
as I stayed picking myself out
from inside a draft.

Cigarette smoke made curtains
over Saturday afternoon's football results,
his thin fingers rummaging
through that tawny beard
as if searching
for the good luck he'd lost
to the abrupt knock of his journey.

Absently
he would walk me to wherever,
our footsteps chipping away at the grey silence
as if the irritating wind
and then playful rain
marred those beloved glasses of his.

I can still hear those football results
I can still hear those Saturday afternoons

when I held his hand just to listen to him curse
the childish season that only wished to be felt.

My Father's Walk

I shake your hand now
our fingers match

we hug
with men between us
speaking concisely
on politics
your silence
still breaking the bones of my points
with eyes too similar to ever meet.

Soon, your hurtling rage floods forward
to drown the water I drink
hurling us back
with our conversation half spelt
inside the same torn kitchen
I raised my first words in

when your face reminded me
of a fatherless little boy
and your thinning footsteps
were all I had to look up to.

Broken Shells

The truth is a single egg
wishing quietly for a voice
somewhere from within the womb of its time
it waits to be born,
to sing up into the ages as a folk song
that people will recall and say
"yes I know this, I remember this,"
but music is a harmony between silence and love
and courage is the only act which can unlock freedom
opening a new growth, an unfettered gala of true spring
reaching out across classrooms and newspaper sheets
and the auto-cue of straight-eyed anchormen
as every enemy infected by hate
stops to watch the sun
buy back the sky with all its gold!

Yes friends the truth is a single egg
complete as the last word placed at the end of the longest poem
it's there, as a mother is, as a mountain is,
and from its permanence it watches us only to weep
us who fight, who thrust our wickedness into the core of days,
us who invent death, destroying the fleece of our world
so we can build dust on top of dust, superfluous graves hanging,
forgotten cemeteries that lean into unrest and the truth
buried beneath it all.

In the resplendent colours of a dream
it clings onto the imagination for life
pulling against the scrawl of some midnight scholar
who writes maniacally I won't forget you,
you didn't happen just to die.

So the truth becomes a dream
swimming within the cognisance
of scholarship and poetry
wandering as an orphan amidst the blur of the true
and the untrue
the opposition vs. the motion
the information against the misinformation
because the truth is a single egg
and a lie is a million sperm
racing to undo it
beating against its weathered shell
with ego, deceit and corruption
until it can no longer withstand the onslaught
and a lie eventually permeates the truth.

A young boy came and sat beside me
on an old bench where I was writing this.
Peering over into my notebook he said,
"your handwriting is similar to mine."
"Really? Well I'm writing a poem about the truth" I said
he laughed like good luck with that
"I would help you but I don't know much about the truth."
"Well that's a lie" I said, "here, finish it."
"You serious?"
"Sure."
"OK."

When I come home and my mum says she missed me
or my best mate whose dad beats him for no good reason says,
"dude, on your next birthday can we blow out the candles
together?" Or when I step off an aeroplane
and my granddad ruffles my hair
kissing my forehead at the airport
or I brush past Stephanie from the year above
letting her sweet smell pin me to the floor
I reckon truth has something to do with that.

And when I'm scared, like really scared,
scared to even open my eyes
I think of all those kids who'll never open their eyes again
and I soar high for them all.

Still, the one thing about truth that really gets me
is when Sundays come my mum she boils me an egg
putting it in front of me she says,
"you'll need to be patient with how you approach this,
delicate with how you open this,
because its contents is soft and sensitive
some can handle it
others ruin it before they get a chance to know what it is
but you, you will know how to treat this egg."

Handing the book back to me
I ask out of interest "why the egg thing?"
Biting on his nails he says
"you know I think my mum uses that
because she used to love a guy who always said
that the truth is a single egg
and a lie is a million sperm
I guess she was right
because I've never met him."

Glasses

I always spoke to your glasses
the heavily tinted ones, taciturn and stoic.

I had so many questions for your mind and mouth
but instead you just turned your glasses on me

so now I see all I need to see
without the need for glasses.

Talent

The old lady who lost her old man
sat with me on the park memorial bench —
the one with the rusted
In Loving Memory plaque.

She would turn a patient ring around
her forth finger in the same soft way
she would tune her radio in
to listen to her afternoon stories.

I would hold in my hand some heavy book
she'd already lived

then after a chapter of silence she would say
how soon she would die. That she's not afraid.
That she knows people far more fearful
who did it exceptionally well.

"Then that is a kind of talent" I remarked
to the live side of her face where
the waning beams of October sunlight
fought hard to try and protect.

"Talent my dear is not found in fearless dying
talent is found in surviving to die."

Lose My Voice

I could lose my voice to you
in a crushing heartbeat on a stale hospital bed
with plastic veins trembling inside those parts of me
that you would once sink into
to try and find an unresolved part of yourself.

In a flurry of pale words I might sound like a prayer
being led to the end of the world's last bible
only to find that those final few pages were missing
and that God was just a quiet bit of white space
sitting with everything that's ever been said
and everything that's ever been lost.

My fading eyes might resemble those unplugged stars
that would once nourish your world with a light
I would kindle from the beams of an old love,
the same light that once upon a youth came between our kisses
the kind that the moon would try to get between
so as to place itself inside a moment of tenderness
for it knows somehow that the battle against its stony night
is infinite.

We created a family of memories you and I
the incubating sheets of each year
joining to form a calendar filled with Andrew's first steps
and Stella's first dance, those baby words that must feel
like the voice of one dead coming back to touch the heart
of his beloved for the last time
our children are complete islands that persuade that moment
when the soul abandons itself in a burning cathedral
to rise up and breathe again the cool sun of life.

Close yourself to this deflated loaf and just feel my words
because my mouth has been defeated of its only use
and my body has at last forgotten itself;
the strength it once lifted
the miles it so easily trampled on
have now all surrounded me in a reckless grope
fragility is a confine that I pray you never know,
it's an open cell free of its lock,
it's an imagination being held hostage by a broken wheelchair,
it's watching everything grow wild
whilst you're forced to shrink further into yourself
but love, love is an indefatigable celebration
the only hand that can never fold because right now
in this hospital room
amongst these hanging wires
and this air that tortures my heavy lungs
love is the only medicine I have.
So come close and put your hand inside mine
so I can hold again the long fingers of tomorrow;
my skin runs ashamed by the breath that keeps all this poison
for itself so take from me all the words you'll need
to write the poem that if death is to style my little future
I know will follow.

I could lose my voice to you
if you could somehow lose your death to me,
let me take you from that room where unconvinced flowers
bow in their vase as if they too had peered into my heart
and become stricken by its long lament
and in return you could take from me this voice,
these words and this gift
that now sound like a promise losing faith in its deepest conviction
but if I had known
that your last few words would have sounded like they did
and your body would have convulsed and stiffened
as white coats came rushing past me

then maybe I could have thought of something
more beautiful to say,
maybe I could have read you the poem I was writing
whilst you slept under a stuttering beep
that allowed life to meet you through a thinning tube
and maybe just maybe,
we could have shared that last bit of white space together
but instead, all I could do was drown in the storm you gave my eyes
throwing myself into the arms of a doctor
who repeated the word brave without even looking at me
then gave me a card with a number I should call
if things ever got too much.

Your room is clean now my love
no more machines, no more encouraging smiles,
no more waiting flowers.

By tomorrow no doubt there will be another loved one
fighting their last battle against the precious air,
and there will be more husbands, more sons and more daughters
who'll write poems under a stuttering beep
because they don't know any other way of coming to terms
with the tragedy of life's final act

I just hope that they reach the end in peace
because you were the poem I couldn't save
and this was the voice I couldn't lose.

when the circus
is full of clowns

nobody stops to the
think about the lion

On Exit

What is hell but another rich city?

Each way begs to enter
but the only exit belongs to the muddy ground.

Billboards tell you everything you will never need to know
and oversexed girls make mountains look young,
the rush sweeps tying lives together
as the machine prowls our dreams
filling them with immortal batteries.

It's hard on the eyes
a carnival of pregnant sorrow
the consumer is the consumed
as the poet's pen moves to dead-drum rhythms,
sour tunnels of light turning to melt over graffiti walls,
we're all stuck in a London signature
living with these hyper-sirens in a culture that yells
take but never return.

See how the sky looks down on us,
the earth jolts with cocaine at its feet
its skeleton a branded rifle,
its pedagogue bleeding ideas into the future's ill frame
humanity a concept debatable.

For once give me the news without the lies
so as to leave each page lost for words,
each caption a saintly blank,
show me a revolution that doesn't end on a Sunday
and start again next Saturday.

Where is he that will save the life
of a child different from his?

Can socialism exist without the champagne?

There are babies with crayon hearts
making weapons from weeping flowers,
there are babies that will be dead
by the time this poem ends
because every struggle is a repeating sentence
that murdered its full stop.

I would pray but heaven blew itself up in its last war,
I would fight but the real enemy is never seen,
turn away from these towers and fumes,
from this years rhetoric
and leave it all to dance inside its flame.

All things make rust eventually
as the tender good die unwritten
so long
these are the last days
as never before has there been a more
violent group of man.

The flags are all wounded,
the borders lay spineless
leaving the greatest famine to exist
inside the disaster of corrupt hearts.

Love me beyond an ending

                                    she told me
                            I was kicking stones
                               in my head again
                                    she told me
                    I bring the distance too close

                    so take me to where fairy-tales
                          are woven on beaches
                       where waves can die happy
                                    in the sand
        and your pen doesn't move anymore.

Take me to where I can see it all
from the eyes of a genius,
from the eyes of a child,
and on exit leave the world
to make trophies from its despair

so close the door
because here you're safe
here the writing sleeps.

Two Syllables
Six Letters

It's better to not go back to the village,
the subverted paradise silent
in the shatter of shrapnel

— Ramon Lopez Velarde

Two syllables six letters
nailed to the sea.

An island at ease
the cool definite running of waves,
I climb through the smell of its thirsty earth,
its lazy olive trees and poised monasteries
that beguile an unsatisfied God.

Trek deeper, past the cologne of orange groves,
the hacked meats and leaking salads
where a constellation of bruised rocks hurt for its history —
there you'll find it weighing like smoke on the back
of some old donkey forgotten in its dystrophy.

A donkey who bore the strain of injustice,
whose hooves quietly bled while the morally
good gripped the hand of every struggle
but his. The liberals and philanthropists helped
move every preposterous volcano, loaded
with effort to block the stampede of empire,
of colonialism and genocide,
but our dear donkey,
the one who dreamt of a simple clean moon
became too familiar with blood —

his journey laden
with misfortune but still he went on.

United with his brothers
united with his sisters
even when the winter rains ceased to dampen
the tops of the Levant,
the summer sun ceased to shine
and started instead to burn
and the autumnal wind carried within it
the puked stench of a gutted village,
but still donkey went on.

Around he saw his island's scabbed pyrite
exposed like the earth's entrails.
Wine dripped from wooden tables.
Blood dripped from wooden tables
and everywhere was ending.

But that was then
in a time when donkeys were punished
for their grieving,
when the pestilence came to test beaches,
the pride and character.

This is a time they would rather have us forget
but way down in our villages, estranged and plain
there were a few who fought to restore what once was
who craved peace
who sang loud the song of their mouths

that of an island

two syllables
six letters
nailed to the sea.

Old Palestine

Old Palestine is on fire:

From a distance
it smoulders at the knees
fading with a dark flint
into a memory of holes, of gaps
of inertia.

We know Palestine
but we do not know Palestine.

Cemeteries know Palestine,
ones where bent mothers
howl into the earth
like God has always been a little boy
sleeping underground.

Bullets know Palestine,
charged thieves that spark to wreck
a shepherd's simple dream,
a mother's garden pride,
a father's living-room chair.

Rubble knows Palestine,
homes where village windows lament
their shattered vision
and exploded bricks lay in a cluster
over unburied bodies.

Soldiers know Palestine,
ruthless sharks that boast
with the apparatus of carnage,

gutless misanthropes,
racists of dead skin.

Injustice knows Palestine,
trails of refugees swelling up the red soil
like borders where instruments come to bury
their last songs, prayers question their palms
and yes

grief knows Palestine
pushing it back to the temperature that burns
everything but the pale tyrant
everything but the sea
everything but repetition

and the Congo knows Palestine,
Sierra Leone knows Palestine,
Afghanistan knows Palestine,
Iraq knows Palestine,
Haiti knows Palestine

but we do not, we choose instead
to turn away, to forfeit those ancient roses
for the damp simplicity of a million weeds
because without truly knowing
there can be nothing to remember.

The Master's Revenge

There will be revenge
but it will be different from yours
it won't involve blood or murder
or deception
it won't turn sophisticated people to rubble
then call them underdeveloped, primitive and backwards
it won't need military budgets,
fear, prejudice or gender oppression
it will be simple, uncomfortable
and absolute
it will present itself calmly
there will be no screams
there will be no protests
just this:

You are the owner of all energy
needed to destroy or create worlds
within you lies the peace of Akhenaton
the vision of Imhotep
we can go further
the first messiah
you are the writer of knowledge
the keeper of truth
it's looking at you through the stones
in the history of the mountains
and the DNA of the earth
you're there
this wicked narrative is new
it's evil and unwell

1000 years ago you were teaching them
they were lost, barbaric, never knowing
the evolution of language
of culture the influence you had
you still have, you must have
because you're far from dead
listen
to the speakers, the knowers,
the ones who tell you to open pages
and find yourself there,
reinvent the past
pay the oppressor little mind
little mind fear genius
because it knows your story
it knows about the Old Kingdom
and the middle periods
from Moorish Spain to Muslim medicine
it knows about African mathematicians
and the stone calendar circles of Nabta Playa
it knows, that's why it denies
that's why it tells you to kill yourself
death has many faces
if something is made ill
why swallow it?
Don't accept it, renounce it and go back
to before the chattel
the division and genocide
before the White Jesus,
before the Crusades
and the foreign religions that came with priests
and swords
discover the hidden world
because history is self-serving
self-fulfilling, look in the prisons
look in the armies,
look in the places filled with the broken,

the destitute, the trampled on
the us but not them
look and see what happens when you
become apathetic
when revenge is just for radicals
when you believe the story they tell you
when your only weapon is a gun,
when your only hope is a fantasy,
when your knowledge is obsolete,
when your woman is a bitch,
when your brother is a threat,
and your oppressor is your master,
your standard, your ideal
don't ask for mercy
it won't be given
lock it off, leave it there,
it's dead, it's done
the damage consecrated the sickness
it doesn't work
so start again
with just this:

When they ask you for a beginning
teach them about the Grimaldi
about Menes and the first dynasty.

When they ask you about women
speak to them of Isis, of Hatshepsut and Cleopatra.

When they ask you about European languages
refer them to Coptic and Western Semitic
tongues, explain how 50% of the Greek lexicon
is comprised of a Non-Indo European language
give examples

when they ridicule you for saying *init*
claiming the word as being
Jamaican patois let them know that it's
a contraction of isn't it, which is a contraction
of is it not, which is English and not patois is it not?

When they ask you about war and peace
inform them that the word war comes from the
Old English *wyrre* meaning to bring into confusion.

Mention the Golden Age of Egypt,
communicate the fact that civilizations
which have experienced the greatest periods of peace
have been matriarchal - say that twice.

Include the fact that 70% of Native Americans
did not ever wage war with each other,
refer them to Conquest: Sexual Violence
and American Indian Genocide by Andrea Smith
keep close to mind the Haitian revolution,
Toussaint L'ouverture and Dessaline
if they interject calling you Afrocentric or a conspiracy theorist
reply with these names:-
Volny, Gerald Massy, Martin Bernal,
Bouavl and Brophy
continue

discuss human nature, how we remain
products of our environment, how we mirror what we see,
how certain genes are activated or deactivated
in our childhood
determining who we become later,

explain what you mean by White Supremacy
as a political tool to divide and undermine
those who don't fit the aesthetic

discuss Thomas Spence
and the making of the English working class
look at denigrate families in the US and Anthony Stokes

speak of Palestine with courage
declare that before the 15th May 1948 Zionists
had already expelled 250,000 Palestinians

emphasize that people are not born bad
that before capitalism and feudalism
communalism was how we lived
not primitive but equal.

Do not negate your woman. There is more to feminism
than her physical appearance, you may wish to talk about
Simone De Beauvoir, Bell Hooks and Angela Davis
then poetry,

the spoken word that predates the written word
oral tradition, art and storytelling.

Speak until the sun has risen and set a thousand times
wear the crown that doesn't need a stolen jewel to shine,
assure them that you are made from love
that you speak from love
because that is from where you were born

play them a song, read them a haiku
teach them how to dance

many will laugh at you
many will brand you insane
yet when has madness ever really mattered here?

Some will listen, some will stay
and you will grow into friends,
into solidarity, into the forever
we dream about

so treasure your woman
treasure your man
because we're all we have

peace is the master's revenge
so stand in the present, draw for the future
and shoot with all the ammunition of the past.

Dialectics

I'm talking about the young brothers
bunched together under broken street lights
walking backwards into shadows
because for some
shadows are safer than cells.

Young brothers
who don't believe knowledge will pay
like the grams they keep close to their side
with the stripes on their tracksuit bottoms
that balloon over those skinny legs
forced to carry society's failures
brothers
that learnt to hate before they learnt to say
their fathers' name,
adopting a killer's pose to try and conceal
everything they've been through
from windows to hospital wards
to meat-wagons to "watch,
if I see him again"
young brothers
who prey on young sisters
whose faces are far too beautiful for these unnatural streets
sisters who just want to play
but grow up knowing what a blow job is
and what an abortion entails
and what crack smells like
and the precise angle that a head should be tilted at
in order to stop a broken nose from bleeding
sisters who only ever wanted to love their brothers
who envied Cinderella not because she found her prince
but because her's was a story they had to read alone.

I'm wondering about the abusers
who sit in decaying rooms
with dead bodies that hang for curtains

blocking out the arms of the day
as rotten eyes chase a tail of smoke
in some poor attempt to defeat reality,
where depression comes in crisp shopping bags
or stiff price tags
and graffiti scarred lifts that refuse to leave the ground
where windows in their uniform
all appear to be bleeding with rain.

I'm thinking about the writers
who stay awake talking to their suffering
in a private notepad the colour of God
while the tall and healthy sleep inside visions of grandeur
and the tabloid print machines spit out tomorrow's
foreign enemies —
he writes to the pulse of a dying heart
in a cryptic tongue
that teachers will later call unintelligent
and undesirable but his friends all get it
as they take his words and shoot them to the sky
until the night our young writer
tried to save a sister
from getting her nose broken by an overzealous boyfriend
sirens chopping up the limbs of night
the story writes itself from here on
because justice can only be justified by the most unjust
and so he received eighteen months for resisting arrest.

I'm howling about the system
that denies people their history
and teaches racism in all the correct places
that hetro-patriarchal menace
that strips women of their natural cloth
giving them instead a perverted flashlight
to blind themselves with.

I'm beating my fists against capitalism
for the slum dwellers from the heavy skies of Mumbai
to Cape Town from the paradise lost in Chagos
and back round to Rio it's all blood for gold,

blood for coltan, blood for diamonds and blood for oil
blood, the only resource expendable
where poverty's a man-made condition
and slavery doesn't need chains and whips to function
and just because people aren't hanging anymore
that doesn't mean that the idea of White Supremacy
was buried with Willy Lynch and George Washington
there is silent murder in these supposed times of equality.

I'm writing about the broken hearted
the ones whose life has turned in on them
who have only ever known loss
because they couldn't pay bills
and her idea of love was sold to her
by a magazine dressed in bright chandeliers,
to the ones who eat alone in a room made of memories
because they weren't afraid to say I love you
but on occasions love dies before it's born.

Yes I'm speaking about the elderly
who've come full circle to be reacquainted with infancy
the ones who need a steady hand, a clear pair of eyes
or warmth they can afford.

So in the end
I'm left talking about the artists
the ones who salvage the human spirit
who on some days don't want to write,
or sing, or act, or paint or dance
who want to leave their suffering alone for a moment
just to imagine what birds must feel like
when the summer opens up the gates to its sky,
to give their skin to the body of a quiet stream
or maybe just to hold the hand of a stranger
but that's only on some days
because on most days the world beats art into us
and it's always the brave few
who go on to save a billion desperate lives.

If I Told You

What if I told you that all life is African?

What if I told you that the oldest human culture
developed in Katanga Congo

or what if I told you that the Ethiopian Australopithecus
known as Lucy is also known as Dinquinesh?

What if I told you that every Black face is the descendent
of an Ancient Egyptian
or that no country has as many pyramids as Sudan?

What if I spoke about the library in Kemet
and Alexander's pillaging of knowledge,
the burning of books, of culture and philosophy?

What if I told you that the Vikings
were the most pre-eminent slave owners
and that the 11th century saw Dublin
as the slave capital of the world?

Would you believe me if I told you
that White people enslaved their own kind first
or that St. Patrick was a run-away slave —
a drapetomaniac?

What If I told you that Pythagoras was taught
by some smooth faced Egyptians,
as was Thales and Anaxamander?

What if I explained Egyptian Mystery Schools to you?

What if I told you that all classic European philosophers
were trained by Black Africans in Ionia

or what if I told you what Herodotus said about the Colchians?

What if I told you what Ghandi said about Western civilisation?

What if I told you about Europe's dark ages
and how they sat in comparison to the empires of Mali and Kush?

What if you knew about Abubakari II?

What if I told you that Columbus never stepped foot
on American soil and that Africans were navigating the globe
with papyrus-reed ships in 2600BC?

What if you knew about Cheop boats
and that Europeans didn't have a concept for latitude or longitude
until the 18th century?

What if I told you that racism was invented?

What if I told you that we only ever oppress those who are powerful?

What if I told you that in the 16th and 17th century
White indentured servants and Black slaves
fought subjugation together?

What if I told you about J.F. Blumenbach and his obsession
with racial purity and White slave women?

What if you knew about David Walker's Appeal?

What if I told you what Columbus said
when he first saw Arawak Indians in the Bahamas?

What if I told you about the suggestion
made by priest Bartolomé de Las Casas
then what if I told you how many lives were lost
to the grin that swept across Columbus's face?

What if I told you that nothing has really changed
and that racism is ever present?

What if I told you about that battle at Wounded Knee in 1890
and the massacre of 300 Native Americans with the Hotchkiss gun?
What if I told you that Native American's today
have a life expectancy of 46?

What if I told you that the enemy is White Supremacy?

What if I didn't care about African history
or the genocide of indigenous people and instead
wrote poems about Winston Churchill, Thomas Jefferson
and Abraham Lincoln and I refrained from talking about
the 54 countries that make up the British commonwealth?

What if I told you that the abolition of slavery
had nothing to do with philanthropy but pure economics?

What if I told you that religion has killed
more people than it's saved and that nothing can buy you peace?

What if I told you that a teacher's job
is to help you understand what you already know?

What if I told you about freedom,
what if I promoted violence instead of self-reliance?

What if I said everyone that looked like you was a killer,
a bomber, a terrorist?

What if I told you that the media lies, that the news is censored
and that everything has an agenda?

What if I told you about Milton Friedman
and the Chicago School of Economics?

What if I told you about Neoliberalism?

What if I told you about Edward Bernays
or that since the invasion of Iraq 110,721
innocent civilians have died nameless?

What if I told you about the systematic imprisonment
of Black and Latino males in America?
What if you knew the worth of every prison inmate?

What if I told you about Francis Galton
and the Eugenics Movement?

What if I told you about NSSM 200?

And what if I quoted Emerson or Thoreau
and I worked on a building site

or I knew that Shakespeare
invented over 1700 words including the word assassination?

What if I was reading The Apology on the bus ride to work
and work happened to be cleaning office toilets?

What if I was ugly but knew how to make her smile?

What if I told you that music is not popular but universal
intelligent noise resonating from the soul of the universe?

What if I told you that in every bit of me, is every bit of you?

And what if I stopped writing for a second, or a week or a year
would I miss something?

What if I told you that love is forgiveness breathing
and every man wants to be held as tightly as every woman does?

What if I told you that we all want to be wanted
and that cruelty is how weak men respond to fear?

What if I told you that the hardest man I'd ever known
loved me the most?

What if I told you the first time I punched someone
I felt strong but the crying that I did that night
introduced me to a weakness I'd never felt before?

What if I told you the first time I kissed a girl
an earthquake found my legs

and each time I get my heart broken
I become a better poet?

What if I told you that a single act of genius
is the result of a thousand failures
and that every master knew nothing at the start?

What if I told you I believe in you,
in your heart and your life?

What if I told you the greatest gift I ever received
was being told I can?

What if I told you that you wrote this?

Now

what if I never told you?

Waiting

I will love you from that home in me
that has always stayed waiting

that home in me that has always
stayed waiting for staying.

on the broken hearted

Some poetry only works

For You, Dear Friend

This is for you, dear friend
trapped in a secret you can't bear to tell
fighting the darkness for a moment of peace
sleepless in your troubles
your drowning depression
as your insides look for a way out,
and the sharp horn pressed coldly
against your hope cries into a silence
only death understands.

I know what it's like
to wash your face and still feel dirty
I know what it's like
to be loved and still feel hated
I know what it's like
to be alone
to see the flames within your own self
doubt your own self
berate your own self
I came close to the closest part
of an ending but I grew to love
the beginnings that fall at the feet of every failure
I thought back,
on all those yesterdays I had collapsed
only to see that today was only possible
because I refused to stay down,
I refused to be the mud,
that part of the earth people walk all over
I let it go, I watched it leave
and I kissed you on the lips because you said
you hadn't felt anything in years,
and we put on a song to dance to until

our bodies were so full of music
that we went to sleep that night in a melody
no instrument could catch,
and you slept in the promise of my arms
dreaming of eagles, infinity and sunshine.

I will never know what it feels like
to cry like you,
I will never know what it's like
to be black, to be a woman,
to be poor and told your whole life
things that make you compose a list
of a million ways to kill yourself.

I won't always be there when the eagle
puts on its boots and comes to seek you out
or when you slam every door or your friends
don't answer the phone
and your mum's left you in tears again.

No I can't always be there
when the beauty that is your face
turns into something unrecognisable,
something far from here,
something that spells words in a thin trail
of melting mascara running down your cheeks
you whisper a goodbye

but when you come close to the closest part of an ending
think of yourself smiling and see the child
throwing bread to the ducks,
see the child opening her presents on Christmas Day,
winning an award, learning to swim,
saying the words I love you and saying them again.

See the child that has done nothing wrong,
that wants to dance and laugh and sing,
see it all as it once was

pure   still   perfect

and keep whatever calm
you find for me because when I come crashing in
reeking of mud and covered in the earth's shoe prints
I'm going to need your heart.

Can you do that for me?

And all I ask from you
is that you keep it together

because you're harder to pick up
when you're in pieces.

Going Inside

She didn't like being touched.
She made that clear from the start.
He said there are a million ways
to go inside.

                                        I've heard that before.

He played her poems,
read her music
the kind he had written on a night
when insects rioted in his mouth,
on the thick terror of anorexic hope
he jabbed out those words using the marrow
of every catastrophe he had fallen beneath

to which her body thawed
and her eyes broke apart
undoing their beautiful
white storm.

I Mean

It wasn't always like this
I mean
I didn't have to be the man to be the man
in a world that loses touch with its fingers
just so it can boast about having bigger hands
I mean
there was a time where you could hold me
and not be conscious about the size of my muscles
or the speed of my car or how well I could fight
but rather your concern was with how long I'd lay beside you
just to tell you things my mouth
was still trying to learn the language to
because just having you there
whilst the rain gave its silver sheen to all things dry
and the couple upstairs
were still afraid to understand one another
when your skin kissed mine in a dark room
held together by candles illuminating the worry
that made my eyes look rich and I would stare
with too much hair on my face into the walls as if
waiting for them to tell me the secret to win back the world
I had lost

I mean

it won't always be like this
I won't always be struggling
and our love won't always be lost inside the pennies
of tomorrow's lucky dip
because hope sustains the soul
and everything I've ever done
I've done under the influence of dreams

like that night when I whispered into your sleeping ear
that life isn't always about following your heart
and not everyone we meet is good
in a world where love is the only war we've yet to wage
and just then, at that point
I think I fell asleep inside you
because you smiled with those unturned eyes
like all things that have ever been loved smile
and I closed the lights holding your hand
in mine hoping that somehow I could take it with me
when I pass so as to have it build the heaven
I would sleep in forever

I mean

I know I'm not an easy man to be with
and I know I'm hard in places where other men are easy
and I'm quiet when really I should be loud like at a party
where everyone looks like an emancipated photograph
and handshakes are strong and plenty
along with the "how you doing? What you working as now?"
and "have you gained weight?"

I mean

I've tried it all
I've been that guy at 3am talking circles with the last drunk
trying to help him find his addiction's weary purpose,
I've stood with empty vodka bottles
waiting in their glass for a lost bus that gave up on its route.
I've spoken with ignorance, I've got angry at the injustices
I have read until my mind's become a blister
filled with all the world's poison
yet when the politics gets too much
and the racism tests my faith in humanity
I lean back into myself and I say

see everything as art,
hear everything as music
and feel everything as love

I mean

when I come through the door like a bitter draft
that fell out the back of winter's long coat
and I see you standing there with a benevolence
common only in things without a self
then I finally start to understand what I mean,
falling asleep inside the streams of your hair
I breathe the ocean again,
I feel my heart beat and sway to the music
of an orchestra conducted by peace
and I remember my name.

I mean

I could write forever
but most of my words fall on water

I mean.

To Be Lonely Always

loneliness
is a troubled conversation I have with myself
resulting in one of us always
leaving

Non-Believer

I asked her
if she would ever lie to me,
if she would ever leave me,
if she'd ever before woken up
with a winter street chasing the summer of her blood

and she asked me if I believed in God

                                        no was my answer
no was hers

                                        I don't believe you
                                        I said

we all need to believe in something
my love
            and for a moment I considered it.

She lay her head on my chest
soothing that part of my face that seemed
to be the most different from hers

I would never hurt you
her palms opened to say

I swear to God.

Impotent Man

watering
plants

the closest
a man
can
ever get

to giving
birth

Counterpart

one

       more

           time
I get to understand my body
as it lays still against yours
beside yours   above yours
           beneath yours
because my body is a stranger I frown upon
after a lone shower
until like love you appear to touch it
in places that have lived dead and foreign
then as if by the snap of magic
I become filled with movement
and spirited recognition until that moment
when you softly sweep back

removing me

from
myself

one

       more

           time

Surgery

Dr. Ahmed said
that he loathed poetry,
removing his surgical mask
from a face that had been awake
since 5am

he said he didn't see its purpose
rinsing his hands under a warm tap
so as to put on a fresh gown
and do it all over again

to make his way back into pain,
into the tumours, the diseases,
the ailments that burn
the lives of hapless strangers —
to lend his God to their healing.

The theatre lights beamed,
his audience cloaked in sedation
waiting to feel the touch
of his poetry again.

The Blind Beggar's Grave

A man living blind nudged me
to assure me he was there

I turned round to see the skull of the world
buried between both his eyes;
a face that expanded like some waterless rice field
his body an oil stain.

Holding his hands out like graves
I peered into their earth
looking for the suffering
language was unable to confirm

then suddenly, in that moment,
unfragranced as the atheistic moon
I felt his breath beg for some small life
while I stood here so full of it

of vision, of talk,
of wild dreams and fresh blood
but I lacked the courage
to look an old blind man straight in the eyes

muttering to himself
I sat frozen inside a blackness
only he knew how to pilot
his way out from

until I let a small note float into him
and in return he kept open the grave

where I would break
into a thousand pieces of shame.

The Science Borrowed From Stars

It began,
we began,
with centuries
of fresh cut water,
of open sky,
sun-light painting the wooden deck
where our toes would be still
to be loved.

Flowers, plenty flowers
that sprayed the yellow room
with a universe of low aromas,
new days proposed to each other,
alive with insomnia,
delicate as birth,
leaping forward with high pitched ideas
we rolled like bits from another earth
growing in each others laughter,
sinking in each others slumber
we lived only to throw darts at time.

Everything was adventure.
Nothing knew how to age.

All days gathered
to see what would come next

it was the dream reworked
it was the long hour coming home.

We couldn't lose
for loving was winning
and games were what happy children
played best.

We would walk arm in arm
sun in moon
catching the sighs of the unfulfilled,
the arguments of the cracked
or rich bachelors spending
loneliness' commission,

the world held open our eyes
ramming its bitter future into our mouths,
we sailed around the hurricane
clinging to transparency,
to air,

the world did not know us
but we knew it as a wounded dog
that needed death.

        I wrote fast, infuriated as if wronged.
        You listened as a leaf does to its season.

The lethal enclosure of solitude.
A space frigid with echo.

        I dreamt the antithesis of dream
        biting down on reticent bones

the tone of loveliness
began to starve itself
my skin subverted
heavy around the mouth,
I noticed the sky less
the hours shrinking
unspoken in a malady of disdain

visitors left snails by my door,
letters remained unopened,
abandoned words,
terrifying mirrors,
the religion of decay
creeping into closed rooms
and the impetuous void
that murders a home.

I lost myself
to the self I lacked
in a bitterness of endings
that are forever being born.

Your voice like broken water.
Your eyes, baskets of unearthed sorrow.

Strength is a weak man's forgotten habit.

Your lips were old stories
I once told myself.

It made no sense
the applause and enquiry
my words being sought to heal
a collection of secrets
shared with strangers,
it made no sense
how beginnings start,
how love starts,
how art starts,
by accident
with the science borrowed from stars

I chased their cosmic miracle
around my study
out into the coiling city
where all anguish coheres
like two pints of suffering

being raised to the same God
drunkenly insane

alone I look for you

                              alone I find you

you love me
until you see me

                                    your body
                            a wound I write to.

Deeper became the unreal
two indifferent lovers
harpooned by absence
tormented by the contours of memory,
the smell of damp shirts,
the festering nest of longing
your face changing
insisting on isolation
your walk laden with bags
conquered by thoughts
ominous as prepared death
we speak to each other
through shadows
wash our plates separately
cold water running
leaving the front door unlocked
at night I scribble I love you
whilst you giggle like a little girl
in your sleep.

                             Madness
this whole planet is founded on madness
in a theatre of tragedy
a forest is ablaze

                                all that remains in a fire
                                are the flames.

From the stone of tunnels
I feel the hate you kiss me with
I pick the glass out
from inside my bloody breath
hoping to find a clear reflection
so I can make us up again.

Walking out into the night
that masculine abyss
I search the hospital of dreams
for the shape your body made
when it missed me,
I think of all the other beings
and I invent myself in them
away from the loneliness,
away from the sound of love dying.

In everything I touch
I feel the mountains of your bones
hold me like the arms of the world
when the universe whispers
every life is your child.

I travel to the summit of your last solstice
parting the troubles and ugly fruits
then I find the best part of a new moon
and I await my turn.

A warm rain falls into my mouth
and the stars begin to drown
I grow into the light
the science borrowed from stars —
stars that are only ever born
to carry the burden of the sky.

Rain In Hanoi

Here
alone
in remembering
                              you
I touch
the scar
you made
                              me
to try
heal
the side of you
I know
still
hurts
like I hurt
like rain
hurts
when it
                              falls
on
careless ground

and also
perhaps
because
tonight of all nights
I really
do miss
being
in
                              love
with your

human.

Backpacker

Names, streets full of names
they shake hands gripping sweat,
greeting each other in the language
they carry there on their imperial tongue

and stories, stories full of manoeuvres
with death, pestilence,
the shits and how they suffered
        without women to be their health

to mop the poison away with kisses
and the eyelashes of lovely heat.
Conversations gambled on blank village ears,
foreign habits that are adopted to try mend

the bleak distances nested in their hearts,
thoughts of a dissipating home at each burning
bend, bamboo chairs to write safety mails
while the gecko hugs his precious wall.

The girl from yesterday sobs for the boy
she lost today, gone to the rapidity of the journey,
the ephemeral gulf of restlessness: all is plural she says
asking to be walked to the shack of my own heartache.

(why do the most spectacular roads lead us
                                  nowhere?)
        I write back to the rain

as more arrive. Vagabonds lost in their frenzied Bohemia,
hedonists chased by the lustral tassels of utopia,
exhilarated students naive and pathetically groomed

coagulate into familiarity until soon they mutter
where did you come from? Where are you going?

But if there did exist answers to settle such questions
then every backpack would be as weightless
as a snowflake falling around the air of a star

and with that they spill over again. Fly north or gallop south.
A cigarette is left to burn away against itself,
the girl's sobbing stops,
her gardener-hands scattering tracks to some new
                                        destination

that moves further away from her. Gone.
Back into the windy atmosphere of the great voyage,
double-handed or alone following whatever boom
can frighten hearts into one more shivering miracle

while secretly borrowing each other
to place footsteps over the loneliness
they will spend an entire earth and moon
trying to lose.

A Dinner Candle
And Me

On this night the dinner candle asked
why your chair happened to be so vacant

I could see how alone it looked
that shy lighthouse lifting both opaque shores

I spoke to its lambency in a voice composed of sorrow
a raucous testimony full of wet wine low down

the more I tried to elucidate your leaving
the more it would flicker and squirm beneath the words

shrinking, wasting that splendid stature we both adored
with each syllable that left my mouth

I could not stop even as the bulbs of burning tears
rolled down the side of its soft white body

I could not stop as I watched it become an embarrassed mess
with all anguish eating away at such proud form

a struggling glow was all that remained to say you once loved me
and I too had once loved you so thoroughly

a melting face whose tiny ears were at last swallowed
by the flame of the only story it was unable to light.

Nha Trang City

Fiery streets
that spit horns
burning midnight inside a nest
of wooden stars.

Bikes meeting each other
at a deadly stop seconds before hitting
the heart of the moon's crying tumour

the amputated seller at the end of my road
everyday, every night, everyday, every night
sends the same question
to my same tired answer

a city living around a broken traffic light,
the old lady chews rice with her gums,
a coconut breaks its belly on the road to bleed
poverty smells of rotting fish
and trampled dragon fruit
then the noise, the noise that grows
from inside the immense bark of survival.

Little children leap up to my wandering
with crystal skin and pine-wood eyes
pointing in a dialect I can understand
only as taunt —
I write the word grief
on the face of a 100,000 dong note
hoping they will always remember
to play with whatever they make of it.

Passing the squatting mechanics
sparks massacre the air's fragile pupils,
metal makes love to more metal,
a half dog chases the ghost of a famished cat,
a lizard sits on the side of the road
waiting for Buddha to show
as the shirtless peasant pisses
a dead yellow river while vomiting up
all that he wished he could hold
like an organ within.

All these signs, tokens of metaphysics
peak the nettled quality of my dismay

and again I think of you, sitting without me,
drinking a light drink, surrounded by cakes
and friends who make you laugh until the table shakes
and you get the sudden urge to dance
to music I always said lacked soul
and good earth.

I have come away to find you once more
to the pallid throne of memory
because home has left me.

On the night we spoke about suicide
I insisted that there was nothing more dangerous
than an ocean watching a troubled man inhale his own silence,

yes my burden is hostage to a sack of poems
I tremble to read back
overladen with meaning I try to rattle them off
as fiction, as pretend, as plastic,
but none of this holds use, the ocean knows
for it has seen many strong men
become broken by sand.

This magnificent ocean
—ancient sky of ground—
I can see those green hills
of gypsy glass carry the secrets
placed upon them back into that deep solicitude,
that watery dune,
I can see how the ocean is imperishable,
how in war it can never be
destroyed, dismembered or rearranged,
how lions cower to its roar,
how ships of the sophisticate
become grammar on a page.

I see many things as the surf falls in
with its elated gleam fixed on its silver lips
bequeathed with the blessings of warm salt-water

then I notice that with each strike of wave
the mighty shore only ever moves into the path of its dying
as it lives on shrinking
in its own golden loneliness.

From
A
Sad Dance

2011

Truth & Beauty

We suffer from some unknown place,
from a dark pit where we circle
ourselves as loneliness, despair and mistrust.

It is there we enter to stay
roaming lost in a tumult of contempt
until our will alters the shape of the pit

and the hard circle which contains us
slowly learns to forgive
until it parts to release

ourselves from ourselves.

Refugee

When I come to love
I make the shape of an old bench,
a solitary platform whose surroundings
are built by echo.

Darling woman, body of topless sky,
spin into my faint mood and swim with me,
lend to my fears your softest feet and dreams
for they fall into my eyes as a singular joy.

Away from you I am old hair
making my way around the troubled world,
as clothing that no longer fits the design of growing life.

Look at me as one stray dog
broken uneven by his skinny bark
stuttering in this atmosphere of spitting coal

for when loneliness finds me I'm always with myself
holding on to some inanimate part of you
like the sheets of a bed
or the baked air that craves a window's mouth.

I am always the man I never wanted to be
unsure as any beginning
and at times sadder than the close
of something that filled the senses with the lift of birds.

I pound against my flesh all that doesn't exist
until peering over the world I see you
turning sweetly into the nearest ocean
holding all it loves close to its mass.

I see you as all beautiful things should be seen
as salvation, as touch, as poetry

I see you as my middle and you see me
clambering towards you as my end.

The Funeral

Poetry doesn't belong to
those who write it,
but those who need it
— Il Postino

There was earth all around
dark rich earth that spread itself completely like blindness.

There were branches divorced from their fervent summer springs
and there was rain, there's always rain,
long devout crystals of melancholy
which drip off the corners of umbrellas
still as November crows.

Between the space of life and after life
a neat hole lay deep before us —
final and rapacious.

Within it will soon be returned the breath once borrowed
delicately reaching as the exchange of two gifts
a box enclosed with a million stories slipping below
past our beaten eyes and beyond our feet.

I watched over the sobbing murmurs of women perfectly crumpled,
the tissues absorbing the deep mourn
which binds as a ring's seal and my shoulder naked again,
my sadness alive and afraid.

Further he fell along with the memory contained within
like a rigid plank we gave him with reluctant hands,
a poor confession at the tip of our prayers

and like everything time made his indelible bed real.

The consternation of the helpless grew
as he passed each grave mark
lower, lower
until softly his bones surrendered to the wet mud.

The rain fell violently on black shoes
gradually becoming tears,
bodies of loss, the chimes met the wind
and our hearts all at once forgave.

At that last moment I glared into the faces now deformed,
those that were future-bound and firm,
those ordained by wealth, with hands like pillows
settled by luxury and there I saw the futility of it all.

The last prayer given to a place unfathomable
the crowd like the name of the one interred would slowly fade
untying the unity that death lends the ephemeral black dress.

I remained as the last
arresting the tears which swung under my eyes
like bells too afraid to ring through the suffering
that sustained them.

I held onto myself
throwing a faint goodbye
to the ashes and dust that lay asleep on him now

then I hung his most splendid portrait in my heart
turning away to face the world as a promise reborn.

Not The First

This is not the first time I have been below love
nor is yours the first blue I have found to dream in.

Your stadium eyes are not the first to confound me
nor are yours the first fingers to turn my wounds around

but I think you should know

that yours is the first long walk I made with peace,
with the whispering effusions of your settled light

and yours is the first body I felt as my very own
in your quiet title of simple surrender

feeling today becoming forever
and hours becoming all moments

climbing to the summit of your adore
I rejoice like the first champion waving a slow love

all the soul longs for is woven perfectly in the truth
of a touch, in a tight hush where all treasure culminates

and I look to you pulling infancy over me again
for the first time I sprint inside everything real.

A Loved Silence

You found me in a place I had never found myself

opened me without motion but with wide absence
in a frailty only rain could touch.

I found beauty in your rich darkness
there I would wallow as something blind
a thing sitting hurt by you and your harm
ageless, so as to condemn me to time and its infinity.

You looked at me in all end
wanting me to part with the suddenness of lost patience.

I become a long minor note
dragging romance by its useless soul.

Never have I seen how your lips move
only how they forge prisons inside me with their feel,
their cold taste breathing words to poems —
silent words which can only be felt when absorbed.

Something further leaves to understand
there is distance in all sad things.

I Will Not Be There

I will not be there to save you
when death comes smelling of smoke
lowering your name into its nettled palm
where you will fade beside choked sunlight
withered as the shins of winter
where you will give your blue words
to the winds raucous ear.

Nor will I be there when your last son
crawls into a crystal lake
giving his wounds to its sky waters
spreading his death
until he floats on his last agony.

Your wife whose beauty shivers
like a child unwrapping hate
will have her rose ripped from within her
by stern tractor hands,
fingers fornicating in the womb of things that kill
        swords lubricating oblivion.

Beware of monsters with pickled fruits in their mouths:

She too shall make peace on death's roads
filled with shoes and mirrors and kitchens
that weep over threaded bell-towers.

Your father sagacious in golden thread
will be taken to the temperature of all grief
where he will be tied to the intestine of a dead pig
        and fed bats for nights
all until the lost hazel in his solemn eye falls

fixing itself with beautiful blood to a senseless floor.

Instead I can write only about the graves
which look only to torment my comfort with their numbers
graves that ache when forced to give their earth
to such quantum death
      again

     and again

     and again.

Burma Makes Me Bad

We sat there on that boat
whilst the sun bled over the desolation
of a country beaten like a mistake
the waters reflected atrophy
and the sky didn't exist anymore than it did yesterday
every day was broken
weathered by the corruption that erodes
the beauty of the black, the brown, the red and the yellow
people of pale dominance.

Here, in this sector of plasma TVs,
reclining sofas and *News At 10*
that puts your feet up to watch the murder of genes
which is the genocide of generations of geniuses
regardless of gender that genuinely
wanted to engender a better humanity
in pathetic style
        we show compassion

but there in Burma,
in Myanmar,
there was a thick desert that came from the seas
once upon a time
and time doesn't leave
it only attempts to forget but death
is ubiquitous and tattooed,
hunger is full
and oppression builds families
that cuddle up only to evade the marching

boot of power
          outside
poor people always have to suffer
like a mother giving birth inside a manger of flames,
burn with love, burn with indignation
and kiss the forehead of your dead child with ash.

Mother
          Father
                    Brother
living in merciless times
that repeat in every country that champions its bloody art
with trophies of skyscrapers, or neat flags
or anthems that sing in discord over the moment
a nameless hero flings his body in front of his sister's
letting the bullets reshape his chest and skull
just so his spirit can ask death to spare her

the last one left she breathes on
with vultures eclipsing her sun.

Her brother left his still eyes in her memory
and that's what she sleeps with every night
when a white man
socio-path, repulsive and indolent,
opens her legs like the torn pages
of a book she's already read
she knows how it will end and she cries
whilst he goes inside her with the heat and mosquitoes
throwing down the money at the end feeling light
          and rejuvenated
closing the door saying
          I don't know the Burmese for thanks.

We were still sitting on that boat
when a street kid who was no older

than the paper plane he had just made jumped on
he wanted money but the type that could buy him dreams
sold to him in magazines only foreigners could afford to buy
his frayed clothes hung loosely around his shoulders as if
hope was a uniform slowly losing its grip
he winked like a pimp and asked if I liked
hip-hop and McDonalds I said
I write poetry on bad days and don't eat chemistry
he wanted to know more
his mind a void that yearned to know substance
the dirt under his nails lending me their truth
for a moment of empathy
and the dry blood around his lip
made up the flavour of the only food he had ever tasted

I asked him for his name and he paused

the sun was shot dead and the reflection
in his beautiful eyes opened the tyranny
to history's longest funeral

my name is Nigeria, Zambia, Egypt, Australia,
India and Canada, Cyprus and Sudan
my name is Red Cloud and Geronimo
Hototo and Kestejoo meaning slave
meaning nameless in a history of names
that lose recollection to a blank
                space of existence

dissipating back into the oblivion that fate snatched us from
with no thank you, no songs, no God,
just a departure from a time that never
even knew we were here he stopped
                and I held back

maybe a tear, maybe a curse word,

maybe a scream but probably a hug
        and I said with the same tone
that finds the voice of a person who's
trying to reconcile somebody whose mother's just died
        I'm sorry for all this
burying my face in the last shadow of that old boat.

Then, silence

as the captain boarded we prepared to venture back into the ice fist,
the kingpin of war,
the mighty general whose heart has always been a gun,
or a bomb, or a sword or a whip
but I needed to know one final thing
        how comes your English is so good?

Holding his head high he paraphrased Orwell
Burmese Days then said
        "my father was a white man,
        my mother Burmese,
        and now both have left
        both gone from me
        today I want to do good
        but Burma makes me bad
        and here nobody cares for us.

        When we die people expect it — it's fine
        when you die people cry for many years.

        I know history and I know what you did
        I don't know the English for thanks."

When The Last Bomb Falls On Love

All around the wretched fall frail
on graves that balloon as impregnated earth,
a singular cause whirls rampant,
a seed from bitter lime engendering new death.

True it is that some cut souls
never before have been spun by the neat tapestry of love,
true it is that its tender fabric, its cloth of adoration,
remains foreign to their skin,
their temperament fetching comfort
from the choking woes of others.

Often you will see their smile rising
to the brim of an ending
with teeth manicured by decay
as their food, heavy as carrion,
gets brought to them by perilous serfs.

The future becomes all too mute,
its stories lying blank beneath a plain shovel,
there is empathy in all but the long rain
for it only reasons to dampen and wane.

The story is familiar.
Its ending understood from the horizon of forgetfulness.

We corrugate our perception with hurricane truth.

Answer me then

where do the loveless borrow desire from?

How do hands of such precarious death
catch the lithe stream of hair that falls
from their lover's head?

Where do their tears fall if fall at all?

Across the desk and burning sands
havoc finds ways to spread
like a tide of fire ordered by infinity,
the quagmire blooming from horrid imagination,
scurrying to find reality crippling a child's leap
cutting the legs off a legacy,
forfeiting a mother's benevolence

        famous death
all around
          unmasked.

Innocence drooped in strife
(the dead-sex of war)
days of blood and rising bodies fall into one.

Words rot in the mouth,
words such as love, forgive and I do.

Stretched hands meet death stiff
clutching a translucent fate
shrivelling through the slow hours.

Now I can say love is a pact of acquiescent ruin.

The grandiose matrimony of devils with five fingers,
destructive kings,
gardeners of carnage.

War is the most ancient song,
yet few sing well those chords
that play through its tears.

At last will come the instant
when he who propagates smoke
and battle and entrails
will sit beside the solitary tree of life
and regard it as the last temple on earth
the only thing still among things.

He is humanity's cruel monk,
lone destroyer of the heavens
remaining solid and obstinate after his glorious effort
to divorce all things wedded to life.

Damned are the ponds
no longer glimmering in their weather dresses,
the fish laying heavy and still in their transparent graves
the hues of summer darkened
forever mourning.

Gone are the feasts,
gone are the revellers
replaced now by yellow showers
replaced now by eyes drowning in the vast
loss of such beauty.

All around are graves
            his depressed masterpiece.

Every mountain's set with a million bones
            the skeleton of true war
with the dew living petrified on its leaf.

The breast of each rose hangs
as the lost anguish of those who perished under night,
the locks of the jungles are permanently ablaze
its birds missing colour seek refuge
from the inwardness of the sky's cotton clouds.

Day is night and night is whole
            for the longest day.

The sea has lost her voice
her waves break and ebb in low apathy
silenced by the weaponry
of man and mind.

She recalls the old machines
which clothed her for so long
unnatural hunks with steel palms
voyaging upon her weightless back.

She recalls the men that rest now inside her
beautiful, timeless and handsome they fell
crying late tears final as the act
which consumed them,
their mothers' rocking themselves
to the swelling heart of a picture frame.

Music sits beside the hollow guitar
            static
a prisoner to its very strings
each finger that would caress outward its melody
is now dead and unmoving.

Buildings stand as brutal declarations
            images mastered by decadence
and so the grandeur of what was

becomes the apology of what is.

The globe attempts living as a single drop of sympathy.

We discover him again,
our lone destroyer
              politician, banker, priest
who loosens his tie
taking comfort beside the said solitary tree,
his armies finding each their own sin to die with
              because greed is an insatiable cannibal.

Around he sees the children of his thoughts,
the silent violence of his smoke,
the cover up of falling snow.

beneath are stamped the lives undone by his reckoning.

But, there is still love here
albeit a love lost to a scorched paradise
of boots and tanks and power enchaining
              forever,
so standing in the gaunt shadow
he too dies defeated by the wretchedness
which all the while crawled closer
to consume his within.

So he too dies away seeing
how a world drained of love is a mere mass
of whispering sand and sea.

Said Man To Woman

Man said to woman
I will only love you if when I'm angry
you remain as quiet as furniture.

When I am hungry you bring food to my mouth.

When I am tired
the bed a meadow of sleeping geraniums
will be ready.

When you tell me of your past
it must give the impression of seeming dainty
innocent and unmarred.

When you tell me of your dreams
they must resemble garden flowers in a vase
womanly, ornamental, average.

When you tell me of your fears
make sure they remain uncomplicated
and superficial.

When you speak to me of children
speak with vigour
            your words sounding as clean and sharp
            as clean cutlery.

When you tell me of your mistakes
keep them forgiveable and honest.

Keep your tongue straight.

Speak accordingly but in line.
Be assertive when you wish but wish less.

And remember
when I make love to your body
your mind and your life
you will learn the twists and turns of my muscular rage
and my cool winter lightning

your shape will follow mine

      and woman

hold your screams
up until I've become a deflated wreck
      submit, submit, submit and love me
with all the wholeness contained in your
affection.

In such times of grand equality I ask you finally
what must a man do in order for his heart
to bridge itself with a woman's?

Not a thing.

A Sad Dance

The walls talk of a truth
beating a reality mirrors hold hostage.

Time alone in a room with no sound,
littered with unresolved thoughts
preferring night. Plunging into me,
over me, spreading a vicious tide,
erupting in my mouth
                circling
so as never to leave like memory turned bad or
regret masquerading as experience.

I need hospitals but instead I'm given bookshops,
graveyards to die in with a strange God in my heart.
The healing pages turning to face me
with a medicine daring to touch wounds
inflicted by my own disdain.

Poetry is still a hymn sung into the vestiges of self.

My eyes refuse to stand still or perhaps
my mind refuses to comprehend the tragedy of such hard silence.

I recall a charred loss that once closed me like suicide.

I watched love drown itself in the wind's lament
then I buckled in the snow mortified
looking for a grave in such a pretty place
I found only my own ugly fist.

In the flow of years that remind me of a dark water
or a shadow that leans on its beloved night for support

I find
feelings are unspent words
waiting to discover their sentence,
so I stand inside them
scoping through the vastness
trying to make sense of the loss,
wringing the cloth of normality
begging bruised
where on earth is mercy?

The night loses itself repeatedly.

      The morning flaps against the dawn.

The past is a burning painting we try to save with tears.
The future is this, a house of objects
too dead to move.

I saunter back to the beginning,
to those long blinds
and blowing words and space
that fit my body so wholly

with a poem in my pocket
I see everything lost to itself
with a poem in my pocket
I see everything lost to itself.

From Returning Stranger

2010

For The World

Embrace the world
leave nothing but a trail of kisses
so that when you're gone
every person's lips will miss you.

Blank Conversation

She looked glad when I asked her what she did
with a smile she said she did what she loved

then came a pause
        until she asked me what I did

I thought of the pause
        and needed it back

it was true, looking at her drowned me in a sort of empty violence

I paused for us both then replied,

"time."

Discomforted Heart

I saw you leaving with dust as your handkerchief.
Distance falling at your back making a blur of my every sorrow.

Furious rains around a shack
born only to bleed with the hurt of soil beaten by the storm

and I, rocking back and forth with impossible dreams.

Salvation

Love has disappointed the hopes of some
has
tortured the hearts of hundreds
has
shattered the world of thousands
but love has
saved the lives of millions.

Missing

There is a way of living enchained around solitude
the look of neglected milk finding each incurable morning
as listless taps that always seem to drip wearing heels.

The day keeps the face of old wood
shipwrecked on an island with a single tree ablaze,
zealous vampires sweep the floors with a wading army
of reincarnated slaves hunting the tragic moon of thoughts.

The stillness of weeks and shoes waiting obsequiously
by lonely kettle smoke and burnt bread,
the talk of a city outside, the rise of a world with no face
waking with hurried skin to pursue rust and things that will never
speak.

I laze beside long seasons drawing nutrition from the patience of days,
where the phone forfeits its tongue for the rise of a mountain song,
while the rain knocks on my window with the warmest of knuckles.

There is salvation all around in disaster days and blithe water-beds,
glory ascends from flutes brushed by infant air
gently assuaging the madness of eyes.

Yet, no matter how much this grand peace boasts
parading with auspicious strides and feathers
falling from birds of grace
I still feel an aberrant sword pressed coldly against my heart.

Age & Time

They do not have time
I do not have time.

I have given birth to all my past,
now I must wait for the future to come find me
with its six foot earth,
the exact earth that will adjoin me to the hips of those I lost
to used coffins, to siren songs that play on the organ of suffering.

I have been poverty
saw the eyes of Jesus in an olive pip,
felt his skin of bread break into my mouth on the fourth day of hunger.
I have been poverty
so I know its fabric and veneer, its stench and rot
quickly I became the walk of poverty.

My children came as leaping seasons ripe and full of blush
growing into faces that I had long forgotten,
the rebirth of my father-in-law in temperament
my mother-in-law in fragility,
all the ones who failed to stand up against age old -
deep swans who sunk into the night without a wave or a goodbye.

Then came the bombs and everything turned black.

The earth devoured us all.

I remember the sky burning all night
as machine guns gave us a new sound
shattering the splash of our warm waves.

I remember those fallen sandcastles on our golden beaches,

the ones which would stretch out to bring back summer and freedom,
soon to be laying crushed beneath the imprint of a soldier's boot.
Soldiers who spoke in a tongue away from ours
so when it was time to die we wouldn't know
dying stiff against the proud pictures that hung drunk from our homes.

I once believed if I closed my eyes tight enough I could elude my fate
hence why throughout those blazing years I lived with eyes fixed shut
yet still I saw all my sight's blackness with the story stitching itself
to my tongue
pimping my memory with every new nightmare.

The sun would continue to rise and set
between lips and eyes and limestone graves.

My children grew to love
and soon the walks of summer could be seen again.

Every garden became a cathedral,
every inch of soil became a womb,
snails crept from their stiff shells and winked
whilst carrying their load
            tapping at my heart
            returning my pictures.

So life was lived like a rose learning to love its thorns
I see now how we live and die from the inside out.

These final days where my skin melts into my bones
and I feel the floor steal each step I take,
never would I have thought walking could be so frightening
infused with slow blood weary and clotted and lacking good air
it looks now to find its last piece of heart.

On days words are yelled, cracking over my uprooted ears
like whips loaded with fireworks

comprehension ebbs to divorce me,
handing me over to senility, restless with time,
eyes roll back and patience gets cooked in a pan with no oil.

All I understand now is the silence
that brings with it those butterfly memories
imperfect but sailing free from anchor.

Those of my children that would look for life in my breast,
that ran to me through the cruel snow
falling into my apron of stains,
wrapping themselves around my swollen legs
giving my name to their dreams and my love to their every day.

I have been here before drowning comfortably
in the whims of age and time.
All this will soon forget me
wipe me away like anaemic chalk
as the torrents of weeks will send any footprint I leave
into the banks of the crowded ether.

Here in this old chair of acquired stillness
I look down upon my varicose legs
and know my heart is filled with love.
I look down at these dishevelled hands
and know my heart is filled with love.

I look long into my strange face
and know my heart is filled with love.

Today, tomorrow, now, they may not have the time
but I will look upon my drawing grave knowing
how I gave them all of mine.

Drenched In Mountains

Only a few more days
before I traverse again the famous hips of this land,
drown my lungs in perfumes shifting from the earth's breath
in nameless scents yet to fall into words
       I perspire something like God at work.

Only a few more days
before I ravage those long sinuous roads
drinking with mouth and mind from the sun's mighty back,
skating alongside diamond rice fields where a peasant's dream
       lives within its rustic frame.

I let my heart drum with wedding rings on
shadows reaching wide like palm leaves in prayer.

Here in this unmitigated plain which repeats eternally
over obsequious jungles and little planets made from rock,
it all seems to sing in sounds only familiar to prophets and sages
dressed in cloth fetched from truth's fashion.

       I find myself reinvented.

To be painted by a stadium of colours blind and sagacious
with the hot wild reaching for the weight of my spirit.

Here, where I can sit unperturbed with clouds
mice and grandfather gorges
then feel the mighty gaze of dinosaur canyons lean into me
until every great mystery dances, yearning to unveil itself,
brazen and alive like summer mounting paradise.

Revelations bloom from inside the lips of each lotus flower
cascading over the barrenness of my side road meditation

all until I am nothing but another being breathing in golden moments,
drifting in harmony with the wild jasmine and bohemian
        sky.

How rich is this nature which owns me now?
What price could free me from this bark and
this leaf, this space littered with lakes of whispering
peace?

Only a few more days
until I find again the perfect place to dream
from somewhere within the hive of my every sensation
living forever wrapped around magic motorbikes drenched in
mountains.

Tuesday 3.36pm

The green tea sits perfectly still in water's grave
with the temperament of a hearse stretching in quiet languor.

I hear the neighbour next-door
running the blades of his mower
over a receding patch of grass
raising the smell of autumn to my window
lending me an open clock while delivering him the memory
of Sunday long walks with a wife now gone.

School closes its books
kids trample the streets with laughter and sweets
old ladies look for walls
sharp men in suits stitch phones to their ears
buses screech
horns bleat.

A dog barks at the sunlight.

A cloud moves in the sky.

The evening takes over
as the dying year gives new stars
to decorate the trying smile of loneliness.

Everything is lost eventually.

Morning Commotion

I was laying reading in bed one morning
when I heard

Get up now or we're going to be late
Where are those clothes I had
Ready for you last night?
It's too cold to wear that today
Put this on.
I'll have to make you breakfast
Again because yesterday you didn't have any.
Here, hurry up and eat this.
You know if you keep doing that you'll get ill
And I'm getting sick of the doctor's surgery.
Have you taken your vitamins?
Drink your juice.
Oh for God sake, will you move.
Have you got your bag?
What do you mean you can't remember?
I put it by your bed last night.
Fuck sake, wait here...

I heard footsteps punish the staircase.

Right, hurry up or we're going to be late.

I closed the book
glancing out the window
then she turned up to look at me
squinting through those glasses of hers.

I cried
so did she
all the way to the old people's home.

From
Let This Be
The Call

2010

Let This
Be The Call

2010

If ever you want to make worth of life
you need only lift high
the hopes and dreams
of your brothers and sisters.

Let this be the call that stirs peace from its drowse
disseminating its flume over the tyranny
that constructs cemeteries from lives,
that on a day to come libraries will deny
and histories will die to.

Let this be the call that lifts the laden youth
from their books of capital grades,
that bend scholars of the stage
into gypsies wanting to pilfer Truth,
rinsing tears with ice-water lifted from a blue
conservative protocol and a capitalism which rams skyscrapers
into the womb of abundance and prosperity.

Let this be the call opening the ditch
where the dead look for harmony,
where beaten mothers cling to babies flung
down the footsteps of time like blind Madonna's
handing adore over to mute stone
preserving the atmosphere and affairs of unripe death.

Let this be the call that reiterates through lecture halls,
through pubs and hospitals,
pulling apart the chains of rank and colour and divide,
of yours and mine.

Let this be the call that reaches into us all
eliciting a tear for once conceived not by shame
but rather the unbounded concern
of wishes to preserve life,
a natural life which is by truth
the most resplendent of all gold's.

Let this be the call
to women who live under the hammer
of irons and ovens formed from age old bravado,
those constantly strapped down
and told to undress into their femininity,
to spread the chapel of life in the name of a love and intimacy
lacquered in jingoish delight;
women who never felt the long lock of devotion
offer them to shores where waves bend cries
under a calendar of warm rain.

Let this be the call to every wretched pauper
who drinks from the urine waters
of bloated despots, whose eyes are summoned by
slaughter in dreams which lionise cruelty,
who knows only the perennial pestilence that swallows
their every day expelling them into jungles of land
dead with open stomachs that lessen to taste.
Eyes that elude mercy and sustenance
falling quiet inside the gnaw of rat's feast
whilst hunger stays playing
its sad symphony to peace.
Let this be the call to you America
as your bible drips blood from the right to the centre

in fast-food propaganda
and classrooms which stutter in reckoning
like broken assembly lines.
Could it be those black pipes you buried
in glass sands are the same ones that pump
greased murder into your rhetoric?
You coerce your flag waving fools
with a vomit of stars and stripes
striking down humanity with an allegiance to midnight death,
counting the lives of only yours as if God was a retired broker
forever howling mawkish songs.

Let this be the call to you Great Britain
icemen who feed democracy to sharks,
molesting vultures with stale justice,
tainting the essence of your books
with words that repel Truth,
a commonwealth of bitter alcohol
anchored to an addiction that never wins
and the clever serfdom that indentures
your skipping slaves into a servitude
paving the back streets to war
with their own oblivious sweat.

Let this be the call to you
Iraqis
praying beneath a sky that burns
your songs and santurs,
which picks out the backs of your children
with shrapnel and bullet,
wounds turn septic with havoc,
wrenching the final whimper from your wife's dry throat
as she leans over to die beside a dog that nobody knows.
Your protests resonate the sad quarters
of the comfortable world
where in time they fall into a meek anthem wailing in poor sound

until your grounds can only promise a grave
to keep safe the death that names your anguish,
carried hot in the splintered souls of your roaring heroes.

Let this be the call to you Afghans
as your deserts grow bombs and poppies turn white,
as your smoke pipes glow bigger and your beards grow thicker.
Your men bearing the dead-weight of a lost blood line
somewhere shaking on the lips of a trigger and a crushed chess piece,
the silent inertia that finds you before your end
bestowing upon you a rage whose vehemence was taught
by the gurgled groan of a lifetime friend
until all gets given once again to the white night.

Let this be the call to you Aborigines
whose sun-beaten lips crave a foreign poison
subduing your ancient genius
where you leave the philosopher intoxicated inside you
while the architect who should be culling
words to break the crooked days of pirate ships
and Captain Cooks that came to hang your ancestor's spirit
scurries like an epidemic through split veins,
hunted by desperation, as a reticent apartheid
sweeps over the blistered floors of your plains
to sit you down beside a guillotine's edge,
one that beams the reflection of a wickedly wild moon.

Let this be the call to you Native American
people of the First Nation sitting meditatively
draped in eagles that will never soar,
as your scented chants and medicines
run down the barks of antiquity breaking credulously
at the leather boot of a cavalry with knife teeth;
a cavalry which picked apart your sacred grounds
with money-eyed diggers,
unearthing the yellow metal from your burial mounds

wielding it into a cross which they thrust around
your neck,
the same one that would at last
crucify you.

Let this be the call to you Africans
crushed by mountainous plight,
ignited by the white flames of Kemet
where your libraries once read proud
every elusive blank that stole sleep from a pale genius;
reduced now to a bottomless chamber
containing the quiet consternation
of your Menes, your Ramases and your Hatshepsut,
whose Black eyes witnessed pyramids rise
from that first red earth,
whose silk face first felt the opening rhythm of suns
baptise a million religions
lending themselves to spread your Book of the Dead.
How they left you in a funeral
with books that say nothing
in classrooms filled with black boards
while the lesson stays written
in white chalk,
in roads scorched by corruption
and a famine which permeates every noble sense.
Do you know imperial print machines
still spew bile of monsters and savages
while your original man
still feels the weight of every shackled slave
fall upon his tomorrow.

Let this be the call to you Brazilians
whose children sleep in drains
under a sky defeated by diamonds,
where restless wolves howl confessions of the suffering
met with bullets of dissension and batons of civil-force erection,

gate-crashing authority that turns those candy
orphans around, the ones left in streets
amidst pools of sordid dreams
to release a blazing bullet straight into their
unwanted hearts,
snatching with youth the dirt from their palms
then rolling them over to greet forever
in a heap of swollen Black feet that will never dance
at colourful carnivals,
still mouths that will never sing at yellow shirt
football games
and the beat-less pulse that will never love a name;
in a city where Christ The Redeemer
fails the rise to his father's only wish
remaining hopelessly beautiful
at the rusted gate of all those unvoiced
who acquaint forever
an absent
memory.

Let this be the call to you
Palestinians
whose roofs have been eaten by rapine
and skulls
that spin over the tops of riots;
of pleas inflame the knees of widows
and fingers become adjoined by prayers
that sink in an earth tattooed black;
a surrender conquered by the stampede
of troops uniformed by hatred,
married to the gun-whore that roams with open legs
leaving home to be left in the heart
and the heart to be left in the dust.

Let this be the call to you
Cambodians
whose pliant roads still brood mines
that explode over moving limbs,
where killing fields still harvest ghosts
from rice fields that wallow in a melancholy
silence.
Temples, on the heel of the world,
smile with halted eyes,
lamenting temples that once held in their
reflection
an insistence of Rouge
from bodies raucous and slow
fading like useless stars
into the lunar vengeance of
a genocide driven mad by insanity.
Let this be the call to you
Armenians
owners of the Great Crime
that had every hope deported
to an obsessive abyss,
enslaved to the back of a massacre that marches
filling those desolate lungs
with mud and crushed fingers
that never again would plant the seeds
of a fertile tomorrow;
the holocaust rung its dead-bell once again
over the refuge of your apocalypse
deafening the voice of history,
hiding those bandits that snatched children from cradles
so as to indulge the appetite of beasts;
puritans that made graves with speechless flesh
to gloat over their united murder.

Let this be the call to you Chilean
whose great volcanoes failed
to offer indemnity to the fascist atrocities
that drowned each soul in a cold Andean flood.
Whose night never left or turned
to open the face of gems buried beneath your grounds,
as years hurtled your way with rains made from machetes
cutting the root to your Neruda's verse,
bleeding each word back into his beloved ocean
as Pinochet smashed each poor lamp
flickering in your rustic shacks with a mallet
made in America.
Let this be the call to you Cypriot
where your golden farmers were left weeping over their sow
while a mark was etched across your abdomen
like the trail to some drunken caesarean
mauling out the life which kept you whole for so long,
violating the quaint scent of your olive villages,
suffocating the mantra of kicking crickets
with smoke and flying bombers
as the shells fell heavy on the monastery-heart of poor widows
watching as they expired inside drab headscarfs of black remembrance
diminishing beside the rubble of a ghost-home
which on a day stood proud
now to die frameless
as the slaying repeats
until nothing stands proud
nor olive,
nor cricket,
nor wine,
nor sound.

Let this be the call to you
Man of the earth
Woman of the heavens
Child of the future
Capitalists of the skyscraper
Communists of the plough
Nihilists of forever

Black people of the sun
White people of the snow
Brown people of the shade
Mixed people of the all

Hindus of the Gita and Krishna
Jews of the Torah and Abraham
Zoroastrians of the Avesta and Zoroaster
Buddhists of the Dharma and Siddhartha
Taoists of the Tao Te Ching and Lau Tzu
Christians of the Bible and Christ
Muslims of the Koran and Muhammad
Sikhs of the Guru Granth Sahib and Guru Nanak Dev
Atheists of the absolute
Agnostics of the unknown
Spiritualist of the universe

Rich hearts of luxury
Poor hearts of wish

Let this be the call that ends the spread of unnatural tombs
and the schisms which sever the years of humanity
from our hope.
Lives so undeniable yet never will they get to wed
or swim or hear the applause that swirls their hearts.
Stand inside a spine that looks to clear the way
for peace, for justice and equality.

Let this be the final call that says
only when we as a people recognise the ills of the world
as our very own
can we then go forth and make an everlasting change
to all that we here today call home.

From
The Lost
Definition
Of Hope

2010

This Is Us

Life is now - Now is everything - Everything is love - Love is freedom -
Freedom is forgiving - Forgiving is hard - Hard is death - Death is
unknown - Unknown is the future - the Future is fear - Fear is a thief -
Thief is time - Time is psychological - Psychological is achievement -
Achievement is overrated - Overrated is entertainment - Entertainment
distracts - Distractions allow no growth - Growth is knowledge -
Knowledge is strength - Strength is mental - Mental is society - Society
is sick - Sick is man - Man is greed - Greed is discontent - Discontent is
emptiness - Emptiness is more - More is a drug - Drugs are everywhere -
Everywhere is home - Home is safe - Safe is conformity - Conformity
is suicide - Suicide is sin - Sin is control - Control is slavery - Slavery
is not Africa - Africa is ancient - Ancient are pyramids - Pyramids
are Black - Black is Thutmose - Thutmose built empires - Empires
fall - Fall is history - History is invented - Invented is racism - Racism
is ignorance - Ignorance laughs - Laughter is forgetting - Forgetting is
Palestine - Palestine is genocide - Genocide on American Indians are
alcoholics - Alcoholics are Aborigines - Aborigines are few - Few is the
elite - Elite is imperialism - Imperialism is politics - Politics lies - Lies
kill - Killing is business - Business is war - War is profit and Profit is
shared - Shared is inequity - Inequity is suffering - Suffering is real -
Real is corruption - Corruption is money - Money is work - Work is
routine - Routine is dullness - Dullness is the majority - Majority need
truth but Truth is uncomfortable - Uncomfortable is homosexuality -
Homosexuality is natural - Natural is God - God is the sun - the Sun is
existence - Existence is short - Short is devotion - Devotion is religion -
Religion is written - Written is poetry - Poetry is space - Space is
thought - Thought is this and This is us.

London's Dead

And so I leave you behind
 sitting in your quarrels, traffic jams and downpours
 along with the futility of all this:

With your taxes that grow without need
 and your million naked faces,
 your prices and sales of stitched fashion
 that hang in the gallows of blank skulls,
 your concrete rats and overworked workers
 that throw themselves from windows
 nameless slaves that dance with needles in their arms,
 your educated oppressors with their educated impression
  full of class
 telling you who you are to be
  forever.
With your galloping dreams that die
 and snap the child in two
 like the pillage of innocence, the suicide of youth.
 With your promises that suffer from amnesia,
 your injections of rejection that overlap time
 to hand out madness through purple knuckles of fury and walls
 of slashing violence and alcohol that staggers home
 past broken lifts and hearts and burning bonnets
 to fall asleep on The Sun with hands rougher than bricks.
With your perfect smile on everybody's lips
 never afraid in all colours of man welcoming
 yes we can
 the clandestine whispers in only one colour
  superior
 you're all fucking liars!

With your bent rhetoric we all bought for a price unmarked
     in V.A.T. In insurance. In petrol. In blood.
     In diamond happiness,
     in the rainy discourse of the homeless prophets
     who hurl their aching minds
     sitting indignantly against your underground bibles
     in black and white and brown and
     Truth
     in bottles of piss filled with yellow fire
     veins invaded by burnt silver spoon lighters and collapse
     the ataxic pupils who you killed
     with black nails that constantly delve the reality
     of this liberal ignominy stomping on blanketed graves
     and favours the right scholars
     of the right God
     of the right epoch
     that saw many geniuses crumble and pour themselves into sewers
     like shit
     like waste
     like smoke
     like nothing you have ever seen before.

With your trumpeted anthems and frivolous flags.
     Red army. Blue army. Our army. Your army
     hanging from white homes and lives piled on top of one another
     containing the screams of the alloyed night
     as his metal fist pounds her lonely eye
     and then her pregnant belly
     and then her drooping head
     and then the roof of her coffin
     finally.

With your jobless days
    that barren the soul and massage the pauper
    with sandpaper and mortar
    all along those sinuous unemployment lines
    with illegible signatures that repeat hopelessly
    to death.
With your digital way rushing forward
    blinking
    with laptops yes. Televisions yes. Cars yes.
    Phones yes. The bigger the better the cock
    and the bull
    the convenience,
    the lack of sustenance, the loss of flavour and the summer
    and the children playing in the park.
With your flowerless gardens that breathe diesel
    your precious profit and imperilled prophets
    rot together beside the balding wheel of your mighty bus
    and freeze inside fading happy-snaps
    of opulent homes and gates that keep you in
    to keep you out.

With all the solitude of such inherited despair
    I leave you behind as the final grey swirl
    that ascends from the ash of a burning log

and so I leave you behind
like the loneliest picture in the world.

In Three Minutes

In three minutes
a person you do not know will die

Fact:

There in the wretched earth
the shrills of women
dressed in an infinite death
break birds from the sky,
as faceless husbands
brothers
become consummated by bullets
on the street
far from the silk sea,
shells steep the rubble of these bleeding times
slowly
surely
smiles get rumbled from beards
with smoke and spikes,
holy garments cry red
God is waved like a flag in the old playground
where rigid babies lay
with black eyes stitched to eternity,
babies dear God, brown and black,
boots heavy as old iron
crushing sand and sandals with swollen feet,
slitting the throat of an ancient culture
with a tie,
asphyxiating traditions
with proud ideas written in Teflon
and atomic bombs,
blood in the stony wind

beneath the cut debris of homes and welcome mats
explosions
that rattle the night stars
and frighten mountains,
a family fall as a family
              as one
into the mechanical dirt
interred with the scorpions and snakes
in a time that time will bury no doubt
but blood never forgets
running deep into the bones of tomorrow's
unturned children.

So now
a person you know
has just died.

When Friday Drinks

In this month of witches bite
the cold cracks frost,
hours close like a book's quiet end
to awaken monsters with ties and shirts
sharpened bottles
filled with daggers of revelry and storm.

The laughter of ashen teeth
looms outside pub doors
huddled and quick, taking in the poison
of tradition, ignorance and frozen stone;
Watch it stretch itself, a trail of headless smoke
reaching like a starving cloud over moonless rooftops.

The night breeds in blackness,
pumas open the pale canvas
for blood-violence;
men of all sorts savage one another,
brutes dressed in pinks and greens
diamonds sit smug on ears unclean,
throwing lightning bolts
drenched in sallow harm.

Nothing is left as it was;
No brick, nor window
nor sense.

The blue and white wail of the saving anthem
starts as a faint drop of sound
launching itself from beyond the distance,
arriving at the warm red and yellow river
which slithers as an amorphous lake on the ground

butchering the blush of twilight
with its white iron hand.
Polished shoes close roads,
ambulances scatter like startled deer
splintering air.

The crowd evaporates into an early mist
coughing, laughing, hobbling, gone.

Lonely sweepers arrive to pull back
the teeth-like shimmers of a glass and cigarette ends.

Civilisation.

The light-hour turns like an impassive back once again
into another set of something like bright felt-tip pens.
A new day sips its coffee and reads its stuffy headlines,
briefcases and heels open and ascend over last night's stain
like a valley of poor golden chariots rushing into oblivion.

Everything moves except the wind,
        that hangs tainted and low with the solidity of blood,
        the blood which always seems to find
        its long concrete universe when Friday
        turns up to drink.

Slow Boat Ride

It starts to move me over an ocean of frosted glass
held together by the pure flags of every wild season
hoisted proud on the shoulder of clouds
until

                                               space

enough to sustain the appetite of all future
or to accommodate every wild chance
or every possibility that could open either
into a poem or a coffin, and then greater

                                               space

to release dreams from bubbling tiers of white froth
that spill and spit for miles,
enticing me to slip into a momentary absence
like an overdue reverie
spreading its side on the horizon with nature as a float
anchoring me still,
holding my deepest meditation with bridal fingers
if only its darling wasn't so ephemerally inclined.

I have seen you all do it
people of fortune and misfortune,
the loveless and the spoilt.
I have seen the majesty of the ocean
captain your busy minds away

setting free its sail to voyage the waters of your slow hearts.
I have seen the hopeless flattering
in the lonely nets of the fishermen at dawn,
in the languid stroll of the deep peasant
here at the hip of the world.

I have seen those heavy stares
which work to exceed a lifetime
casting themselves into the orphaned distance
hoping to find the dark eyes of eternity

but that is all behind me here
where wave and salt lay bottomless beneath me
until I too become filled with this

                                    space

resting my existence on the shaking fingertip of a wet sky
like a raindrop falling into the bright vein of a rose
or as the first crystal daughter who invents ideas
or when evening comes as the old sorrow which fills church bells
in winter
and lastly with all those blackened stars
who lost the home of their famous constellations

to become perennially part
of all that is missed.

All I Can Write

Never has it been my intention
to bring failure to your door
rather, if I could, I would pilfer a split star
to glide over your small finger
or maybe have your pillow filled with angels
who with hope could secure your every dream.

But being the person I am, inflamed by poetry and madness
I'm able only to bring you my little life's melting earth
along with the damp fabric of all my love
but if you permit
I could try to dress again your lone wounds
in those same simple colours that sweeten funerals.

Nothing Dies, Love

Who now will have to go under your tongue
as you stand him up to kick him down?

Who now will wake beside you to see dawn in full bloom?
The bouquet of your smile in winter's silenced need?

I have been thinking of you alone, then complete,
and it burns like fire-sand.

Who now will have to catch fears
the ones that spring from behind storms and rocks?

Let me see him do it!

Be the man to settle himself in front of your nettle howl
as an avalanche leans heavy and forward.

I have been thinking of you alone, then complete,
and it fills me with new knives.

Just abandon my memory in the undergrowth of all things failed
and I shall take yours to my monastery of dead love
where it will live inside a flame of red and stone time.

But look, if at any hour you should suddenly hear yourself
calling out for what we once were then find me

I'll be scrawling on topless water
nothing that loved can ever die

            on the same edge that once met us both

as the repeating crash of madness
rumbles inside both our secrets.

Love's Epitaph

You who were my everything
cut me down so recklessly,
fixed me out to bleed over grey cold stone

your words splintering my mouth
with grey cold stone;

that shrapnel voice refuting the love
which once came as the laughter of a child.

Bitter perfumed memories trapped
inside these scented sheets
tapping at my weary head
                all night long.

Your pillow's now an open palm
single and exposed
as the colour of crows swiftly ripens
to cremate your absent nakedness.

Strange and forgotten is this infirm feeling of loneliness
sleeping thickly beside me tonight,
edging me forward, daring me to dream.

Smothered by its rank breath of rusted metal
                a lost butterfly inhales fire.

And so the ample night remains firmly severe
for derelict lovers can only hope of sleep
into the womb of years unborn,
into that fertile land where love ferments the soil
and birds dump babies from heaven.

Tonight is truly night
heavy with a thistly ice

daring me to lay a dead flower
beneath the single foot of your name.

From
Card Not
Accepted

2009

Everything

The Rich man sits with nothing but a wallet.
The Model sits with nothing but a mirror.
The Celebrity sits with nothing but an ego.
The Politician sits with nothing but power.

The Drunk sits with nothing but his past.
The Student sits with nothing but hope.
The Philosopher sits with nothing but his thoughts.
The Musician sits with nothing but a note.

The Playboy sits alone.
The Killer sits in violence.
The Adulterer sits in a lie.
The Broken sit in silence.

The Victor sits in glory.
History sits with a story.

Corruption sits in man.
Justice sits at a desk.
The blueprints of this culture sit in the sand.
While the truth looks on in jest.

And I sit here.
With absolutely nothing.
But from within nothing.

I found everything.

Himself

A man stands inside the noise of the world
but all he hears is peace.

A man stands inside the stillness of the virgin field
but all he hears is noise.

All a man ever hears is himself.

Love's Intention

On that very day
the tides of circumstance broke graciously into one another
from the stony shore formed two natural lovers

strolling through ignorance
they waved to its blubber.

On that very day
old man prejudice swallowed his whistle,
drowned in the gossip of all his own people.

Creed happened to forget its crown of thorns
as the sleeping bird sung through the willow
until the night rediscovered the dawn.

On that very day
he turned to speak

'Let me divorce all these flogged traditions
and love you plainly,
take a pin to burst every hollow notion
so as to fill myself with a single purity
like the beginning, the re-birth
I'd rather be held by your timid truth
than by the edges of confection
if only for a starving second

I would rather that than be left to paint forever
in all the colours of the lost and scorned.'

Her eyes still as breeze
                unscathed

as the sound of triumph applauded beauty
for finally revealing its face.
She drew him close enough
so their hearts could touch

she turned to speak:

Love's intention bears no critique
is all she needed to say.

Nike Shoebox

Born within the tomb
of a crack infested womb
no hospitals
just a cold bathroom wall
splattered with filth and fuck.

Geezer cut the cord
with vermin hands,
smacked me hard, lit a fag.
Smoke bending
she's laid out and bleeding bad.

Wrap me in a shit-stained sheet
Nike shoebox turned out
shoved me inside to sleep.

I cry but no one's nearby,
I cry till it hurts,
face burns red feels like it's about to burst.

Absence mothers me
while she sleeps into the days.
Skinny still state
my mind only hours old spirals into haze.

Saturated in neglect
I grow to become faint.

Frozen by reality
in this Nike shoebox
where I cried, shit and coughed.

The baby that time forgot.

In this Nike shoebox
the only thing I ever felt
was my heartbeat stop.

On A Journey

I board with the others
                      I sit to watch
the lady in front
                      eyes kind and suspended
somewhere in last night's moment
                      toying with that little sparkle on her
finger
still smiling at what he told her.

The guy to the right
                      becomes the music wrapped around his
mind
nodding his head as if in agreement
                      wandering through a harmony
found in rhythms of peace.

                      The elderly man
cropped white hair, smoky old shirt and charcoal hands
                      tilts his head back
burying himself
                      in the uncertainties of credit crunches
                      and greased kebabs
(Allahim bana yardim et)

The doors open
                      he leaves she arrives
to the scribble of my pen

heavy pram
          shopping bags
          with
          obese logos hang

scruffy little man eager to roam
her eyes on vacation
lost somewhere unreturning.

    Clutter and noise
big group of boys
        lager streams like wild inhibitions
        old man's shoulders rise into tension.

Look at the floor, we listen to the chaos of small words
        foul mouths which only ignorance ever heard.

Start the chant of glory and triumph
        victory for everyone but them
                    bittersweet men.

Doors open
            my stop
        suits and briefcases swarm
a last look around
            followed by a dot.

Wake

Part 1:

The bird sung
to wake the day.

The clock rattled
to wake the hour.

The door opened
to wake the journey.

The coffee gulped
to wake the man.

The boss stormed in
to wake the deadline.

The phone rang
to wake the deal.

The deal was sealed
which woke the pound.

The applause was heard
waking those on the lower ground.

Part 2:

The champagne was popped
to wake the ovation.

The bar was filled
to wake the party.

The drinks were spilled

to wake the inhibitions.
The coke was sniffed
to wake the high.

The sex was had
to wake the life.

The sleep came last
to wake the rest.

Part 3:

The morning sun broke
to wake reality.

He stumbled off home
to wake his wife.

Strange car outside
which woke his suspicion.

Wine glasses in the lounge
woke the vision.

The walk upstairs
woke his heart.

He opened the bedroom door
to wake the hardest part.

Two tangled lovers
woke his truth.

Softly he closed the door
so as neither of them would move.

Never will he
sleep the same again.

Waters Blue Rivers

*For my great uncle Chris Papandreou
who died in the waters of spring.*

I remember he lay
as cold as November
yet the month was still May.

His breath made no sound,
his eyes met no stare
I shook him around and round
but nothing was lying there.

I began to shiver
As I could feel myself sink
In waters blue rivers
I swear I saw him wink.

The Poet

I take a blank canvas and make of it what I will. I spill my mind like knocked over pots of paint, smearing my ideas deeper and deeper, etching and moulding these delicate intricacies of word and language until finally I see the cool abyss. A world layered with reason and debate, a private tongue for the lonely reader.

You told me to describe but instead I refer. You told me to capture but instead I release. This is an open language, free as the possibility in forever. Bask in whatever opening you see fit. Take from it whatever you need. Think of it only as honesty.

Pardon my flaws and abundant mistakes - I am made of breath and man. I delivered these goods in one broken down truck, loaded from a bottom-less space, assembled by debating reflection. I always work the night shift. When I rise to the smell of the human condition I rummage and refine my way through the hours. Nothing makes sparkling sense. I see anguish, I see noise, I see a failing way forward. I make a note with a cross and some pennies. I look for answers in this heap of crosses. In this heap of pennies. This is who I am.

Society throws me to the side (I'll make a note of that). The people here live fast and hard, (I'll make a note of that too). I'll make a note about making notes whilst no one notices me making notes. I'm invisible, sitting somewhere behind the words being spoken from friend to friend. I told him the other day that true art should evoke not instruct, he looked at me like I was of absent face.

I spend my free time sitting in my shadow just to leave my mind. Chequered walls and water drops ripple through a sickly bulb. I make noises with the silence. Tap my finger against my pulse just to check I haven't missed the last dream. I scribble until I draw but only on a Thursday, doodle until I write, always on a Friday.

One man knocks on the door just to visit. It's Saturday. His world is as empty as a hole. I talk often and much, my words swallowed but never digested. We drink with no cups, when we're done we find it impossible to get up. I sleep deep. I sleep numb.

The day of rest is here. Around is filled with waste and scum, the taste of rotten anxieties and loose hair plague the broken floor. The rain punishes the shattered glass from the outside, it hits with mighty purpose. I can hear nature's honest drum, the anthem of all her fury and dismay. We failed her. Now we will suffer for all our gleaming profit and corporate aesthetics. The vanity of our senseless kind sitting high and smug above the humble clouds, affiliated with the matrimony of fickle architecture. Piercing stone punctures a hole in what was once a perfect blue sky. We ruined ourselves. Sitting in the second I take pen to paper and carve a new message. Roll up Mother Earth I want to breathe her. Here is everything we have ever done, everything we have ever thought.

The present mothers history. The present concludes all human theory and intelligence. The present is endless. Swim in the ideas, explore the abstractions, show them around then let them play. Laying flat on the ceiling I sit in my head, crouched on the floor with my knees tightly bent. Look up. Look down. the (I know, the *t* should be capitalised) phone rings.

I answer to her on the other side, three yeses and a goodbye. She comes over to see me in my experimental state. She looks worn; time tattooed its logo on her face. Her remarks are soft but profound. Her stay brief. Awkward. I hear her ramblings, lips move to the murmur of a dull sound. Words without colour drive me insane. She kisses my cheek. A sign of affection. I could pour out the contents of my heart but the mess would be too great. She hurts me. Once we shared what was precious, now when I need to love I press my lips into the cracked glass of the picture frame she lives in. A moment frozen in someone's eternity, superior to time, running over tenses past and present, this is where she'll stay.

I pick up a pen, rummage through some scrap paper and scrawl the word love. I throw the word out the window - it's neither needed nor welcomed.

I move over to the music box. Lights and digits defining the age. Wires and components giving birth to vibrations so sweet and bliss. I crank the volume to the max looking to find heaven. I want it to attack me. Leave me lifeless and beaten in its wake. I want it to grasp my final foul breath. The sound plummets down on my skinny frame. I fall to the floor bleeding out from the soul. I curl up and crawl behind defeat. I weep for everything I still can't understand.

Acknowledgements:

None of this writing would have been possible if it wasn't for the unfaltering support I received from my parents throughout the years I was trying to establish myself as a poet. Thank you to my partner and best friend Sabrina Mahfouz for lending me such invaluable and benign advice, while also endowing me with the assurance that is sometimes needed to move forward and away from the clutches of self-doubt. To my brother Matthew, sister Stella and aunty Martha for their constant support and friendship. To my close friend and erudite lawyer Louis Karaolis for not just writing a very flattering foreword, but also for our bouts of late night pontificating over cups of green tea. To the indefatigable force that is Joelle Taylor for helping to pull me out from the mess I was in as a teenager, and for her continuing and critical work with many who are now how I once was. To the wonderful Michelle Durham at Whitmore High School, Harrow for allowing me to run my poetry workshops with such an eager and perceptive group of young minds. To the fearless visionary that is Madani Younis at The Bush Theatre for the unparalleled support and belief he's bestowed in my writing over the years. To my good friend Kingslee Daley a.k.a Akala for being one of the first people to endorse my writing back in 2010. To the design wizard that is Ben Lee, thank you for producing yet another beautiful book. Thank you also to the Out-Spoken team – Karim Kamar, John Berkavitch, Sam Bromfield and Assumpta Ozua and finally to my oldest and most sincere friend Phivo, who's always been there even when he's been away.

Thanks. So much.

Anthony

Other titles by Out-Spoken Press:

A Heartful of Fist
Poems from SLAMbassadors 2016

Out-Spoken 2015
An Anthology of Poetry

Titanic
Bridget Minamore

A Silence You Can Carry
Hibaq Osman

A Difficult Place To Be Human
Anthony Anaxagorou

www.anthonyanaxagorou.com
www.outspokenldn.com
www.outspokenldn.com/outspokenpress/